blue & white
cross stitch

blue & white
cross stitch

helena turvey

inspired by the

classic designs of

Willow Pattern,

Delftware and

Toile de Jouy

hamlyn

I dedicate this book to the 'Wise Elders' of the family, to my mother Pepi and step father Lukis, to my father James and my step mother Mavis and to my parents-in-law Marie and Tosh, all of whom I love and respect.

First published in Great Britain in 2001 by
Hamlyn, a division of Octopus Publishing Group Ltd
2–4 Heron Quays, London E14 4JP

Distributed in the United States and Canada by
Sterling Publishing Co., Inc.
387 Park Avenue South, New York, NY 10016-8810

ISBN 0 600 60194 3

A CIP catalogue record for this book is available from
the British Library

Printed and bound in China

10 9 8 7 6 5 4 3 2 1

Contents

Introduction

At some time in their lives, almost everyone has admired, owned or come to treasure blue and white pottery of one style or another. Some go on to become avid collectors, but even if you possess just one or two favourite pieces, these will invariably be displayed on a shelf, dresser or mantelpiece – not tucked away out of sight in a cupboard – so that their beauty can be enjoyed by all.

Why are blue and white ceramics – or, indeed, blue and white designs in any medium – so enduringly popular? Perhaps it is the simplicity of the single-colour design laid on a white background. This makes the patterning, whatever its style, easy on the eye, with a clean, pretty look that appeals to people of all ages and tastes. Designs can range from very straightforward to incredibly intricate, traditional to contemporary, so you can select a style to suit your own preferences and décor.

Beyond this, a number of the traditional designs achieved widespread popularity in their time, spawning myriad variations. Some of these patterns survive to this day – the Chinese Willow Pattern being the best-known example – and familiarity in an interior is always reassuring, making one feel instantly at home.

Translating beautiful blue and white patterns from a wide variety of sources into original designs for cross stitch has been both a daunting task and a privilege. Inspiration came from many different parts of the world and many centuries,

mirroring the rich influences on ceramics that gradually spread from continent to continent.

In the 9th century, fine Chinese porcelain with intricate designs made their way along the silk routes to the Islamic world, at a time when Baghdad was probably the largest city in the world and the creative arts were flourishing. Later, the Safavid dynasty (1499–1736) marked a time of stability for Islam and a distinctive Safavid style of blue and white pottery evolved.

From the 10th century onwards, the Moors from North Africa and Mesopotamia colonized parts of the Iberian peninsula, bringing their decorative blue and white pottery with them – the design style was large and free, typically depicting birds, animals and leaves. From here, and specifically from Majorca, the ceramics were exported to Italy, France and England. Portuguese buildings were decorated with tiles known

as *azulejo*, a Moorish word meaning 'smooth'; later, the blue and white tiles often seen adorning the interiors of their churches and other important buildings were derived from the northern European Delft influence.

At the beginning of the 17th century, two ships docked at Amsterdam with a cargo of blue and white Ming porcelain. Inspired by these new imports, potters in the Netherlands started a thriving ceramics industry based at the Delft potteries, and the name is now famous worldwide. Dutch Delft was then copied by English potters in Liverpool, London and Bristol with slight differences in style, English Delft designs being more childlike and 'plumper' than those of their Dutch peers.

During the 18th and 19th centuries, the production of English blue and white pottery was in full swing, the principal players being Josiah Wedgwood, Josiah Spode and Thomas Minton. Minton imported a wide range of oriental patterns and introduced the Willow Pattern to Spode, who became very successful in the mass production of blue and white ceramics, while the influential Wedgwood remained faithful to hand-decorated earthenware.

In producing the designs for this book, all these have been my influences – along with the single-colour pictorial Toile de Jouy fabric manufactured in England and France in the 18th and 19th centuries, which depicted gloriously romantic scenes involving people, historical events, magnificent buildings,

distant lands, and plenty of flora and fauna. Reflecting the rich and diverse history of blue and white patterning, I have provided a variety of design styles, ranging from small and simple to larger and more complex, so that some projects can be worked quickly and easily while others present more of a challenge. The finished embroideries have then been applied to objects both large and small, for each room of the home. There is also a chapter for projects that make ideal accessories or special gifts.

Read Chapter 6 on materials and techniques before you select a design, purchase materials and start to stitch. Follow the instructions carefully throughout, and you will be rewarded by beautiful blue and white embroideries that will add the perfect finishing touch to your home. Enjoy your stitching!

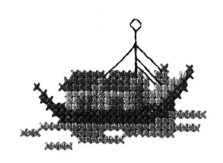

The living room

Are you tired of the same old decorations and furnishings you have been living with for years, but loath to embark on the expense and upheaval that a complete re-design means?

The answer is that you can give your living room an entirely new look simply and inexpensively by revamping soft furnishings with the sophisticated blue and white cross stitch designs in this chapter.

There are cushions in different shapes and sizes, elegant lampshades and a practical teatime tablecloth, all of which will add style to the body of the room, while a simple curtain tie and easy-to-make café curtain will highlight and enhance existing window treatments.

The designs for these subjects are international in their inspiration, taken from Willow Pattern, Toile de Jouy, and Dutch Delft and Portuguese tile designs, but such is the versatility of the blue and white pottery originals that they blend together in seamless harmony.

If you are feeling adventurous, try applying the designs to other items in your living room. Stitch the bolster cushion design as a framed picture to hang on the wall, use the lampshade border on a scatter cushion or two, then apply the café curtain triangles to the edge of the lampshade instead – the possibilties for adding the personal touch to your living space are limitless.

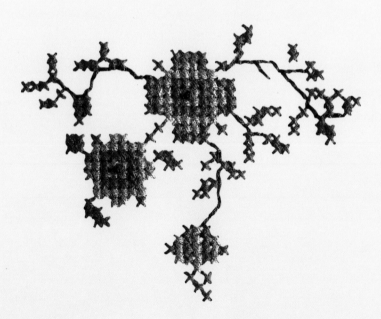

Birds scatter cushion

The two beautifully elegant birds that I embroidered on this linen cushion were inspired by some dark blue and cream plates I found in a local market. The markings on the back of the plates included a representation of a heron, which I used as the starting point for this sophisticated design.

measurements

Worked on 14 count waste canvas, the finished embroidery measures 11.7 x 9.5cm (4⅝ x 3¾in). Use 2 strands of cotton in the needle throughout, and work French knots with 2 twists around the needle.

materials

To work the embroidery:
• Tracing paper for pattern
• Piece of cream linen fabric, 118 x 48cm (46½ x 19in)
• Piece of 14 count waste canvas, 18 x 18cm (7 x 7in)
• Piece of tear-away interfacing, 18 x 18cm (7 x 7in)
• Stranded cotton embroidery threads as specified in the colour key
• Tapestry needle size 24 or 26

To make up the cushion:
• 2 strips of iron-on interfacing, each 48 x 9cm (19 x 3½in)
• 3 large buttons
• 46cm (18in) square cushion pad
• Cream sewing thread
• Basic sewing kit
• Sewing machine

▷

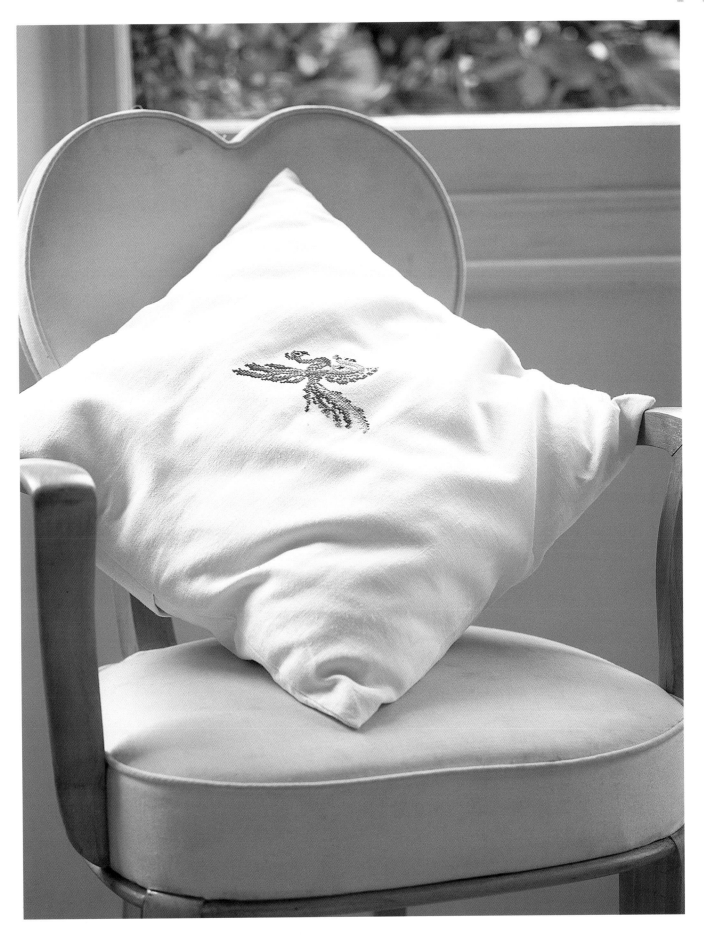

48cm (19in)

1cm (⅜in) seam allowance all round

9cm (3½in)

FACING AREA

1.5cm (⅝in)

buttonhole position

FOLD

12cm (4¾in)   12cm (4¾in)

FOLD

edge of cushion

CENTRE LINE

23cm (9in)

top

CENTRE LINE

centre of embroidery

23cm (9in)

bottom

edge of cushion

FOLD

118cm (46½in)

FOLD

9cm (3½in)

FACING AREA

to work the embroidery

Following the pattern diagram, make a tracing paper pattern for the cushion and use it to cut out the linen fabric for the cushion cover. Tack in the centre point of the embroidery and mark the buttonhole positions using tailor's chalk. Secure the raw edges of the fabric with zigzag stitch.

Prepare the waste canvas and tack it into position, sandwiching the linen fabric between the canvas and the tear-away interfacing (see page 100).

Start stitching at the centre of the design and in the centre of the waste canvas, following the chart. When the stitching is complete, remove the waste canvas and tear-away interfacing (see page 100). To treat the finished embroidery, see page 103.

to make up the cushion cover

Iron the two strips of interfacing onto the wrong side of the facing areas along the two short ends of the embroidered fabric. Fold the seam allowances on the facing areas to the wrong side of the fabric, then pin, tack and press. Fold the 9cm (3½in) facing areas to the wrong side of the fabric, then pin, tack and machine stitch. This process makes the button wraps.

Make the buttonholes to fit the buttons you have chosen, stitching them by hand or machine (see page 105).

With the fabric right side out, lap the button wraps one over the other, with the buttonholes on top. Pin, tack and machine stitch the two ends of the button wraps together. This makes a circle of the cushion cover. Turn the fabric inside out.

Checking that the embroidery is positioned in the centre of the cushion front, pin, tack and machine stitch the two side seams of the cushion cover. Trim the excess fabric from the seam allowances, turn the cover through to the right side and press to neaten.

Mark the positions of the buttons through the buttonholes using a pin, then sew on the buttons.

Insert the cushion pad through the button opening and button up to close.

stranded cottons

DMC	Anchor	Skeins
930	1035	1
931	1034	1
932	343	1
3753	1031	1

French knots

DMC	Anchor	Skeins
● 823	127	1

Backstitch

DMC	Anchor
▬ 823	127

Willow Pattern curtain ties

The design on this ice-cool curtain tie is

taken from the classic Willow Pattern story.

The two lovers are escaping from the wrath

of the girl's Mandarin father by floating

downriver in a boat, looking for a secret

place in which to live.

measurements

Worked on 16 count white Aida, the finished embroidery measures 46 x 9cm (18 x 3½in). Use 2 strands of cotton in the needle throughout, and work French knots with 2 twists around the needle.

materials

(for one curtain tie only)

To work the embroidery:

• Piece of 16 count white Aida, 52.5 x 21.5cm (20¾ x 8½in)

• Stranded cotton embroidery threads as specified in the colour key

• Tapestry needle size 24 or 26

To make up the curtain tie:

• Tracing paper for template

• Piece of medium-weight interlining, 52.5 x 21.5cm (20¾ x 8½in)

• 20cm (8in) length of white cotton tape, 2cm (¾in) wide

• 2 brass rings

• White sewing thread

• Basic sewing kit

• Sewing machine

▷

centre of design ▷

to work the embroidery

Fold the Aida in half lengthways and tack in this centre line. Fold the Aida in half to mark the vertical centre line. Fold the lower half of the fabric in half again lengthways and tack in this line: the point at which it crosses the vertical fold line marks the centre of the embroidery. Tack in the vertical centre line on the lower half of the Aida.

Start stitching at the centre of the design and in the centre of the lower half of the Aida, following the chart. Please note that the borders continue for another 20 squares (not shown above).

Complete embroidery as charts suggest and then carry the border on for another 20 squares on each side. To treat the finished embroidery, see page 103.

to make up the curtain tie

Trace the curtain tie template on page 108 and cut out the curtain tie shape from the embroidered Aida, then secure the raw edges with zigzag stitch. Cut out the interlining in the same way.

Place the interlining on the wrong side of the fabric. Pin the two layers together and tack around

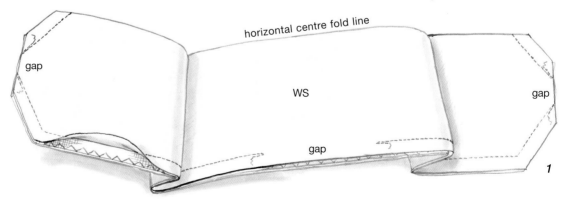

◁ centre of design

the edges. Machine stitch a line just beyond the horizontal centre fold line and towards the back section of the tie, securing the interlining to the embroidered Aida.

Fold the curtain tie in half along the fold line, wrong side out. Pin, tack and machine stitch around the curtain tie, leaving the centre section of each end (where the brass rings will be fixed) free, and leaving a gap of about 7.5cm (3in) through which to pull the tie to the right side (1). Trim the seam allowances and pull the curtain tie through to the right side. The ends, where the

stranded cottons

	DMC	Anchor	Skeins
▨	3752	1032	1
▨	813	130	1
▨	807	168	1
▨	322	146	1
▨	824	132	2
▨	336	150	1

French knots

	DMC	Anchor
●	336	150

Backstitch

	DMC	Anchor
▬	824	132 (boats, birds)
▬	336	150 (border)

brass loops will be fixed, will still have the raw ends showing. Press to neaten. The gap through which you pulled the tie to the right side should also be pressed. Hand stitch it closed for a neat finish.

Cut the cotton tape into 2 equal lengths. For each tape: with right sides together, attach one end of the tape to one of the raw ends of a curtain tie and machine stitch into position (2). Pass the tape through the brass ring and take it to the back of the curtain tie. Fold under the raw end of the tape, cutting off any surplus, and stitch it into position by hand.

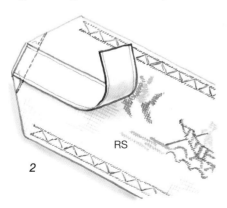

RS

2

18

Bordered lampshade

This design was inspired by a delightful blue and white coffee mug, maker unknown. It would work equally well on a blue lampshade. By repeating the pattern, you can make the embroidered band as long as you like and edge cushion covers, throws or even a pretty waste bin, to match the lampshade.

measurements

Worked on an Aida band (see below), the finished embroidery is 4.2cm (1⅝in) deep, 4 pattern repeats measuring 83cm (32¾in). Use 2 strands of cotton in the needle throughout.

materials

To work the embroidery:
• Cream lampshade of your choice
• Cream Aida band, 5cm (2in) wide with 26 stitches across width
• Stranded cotton embroidery threads as specified in the colour key
• Tapestry needle size 24 or 26
To make up the lampshade:
• Fabric adhesive
• Cream sewing thread
• Basic sewing kit
• Sewing machine

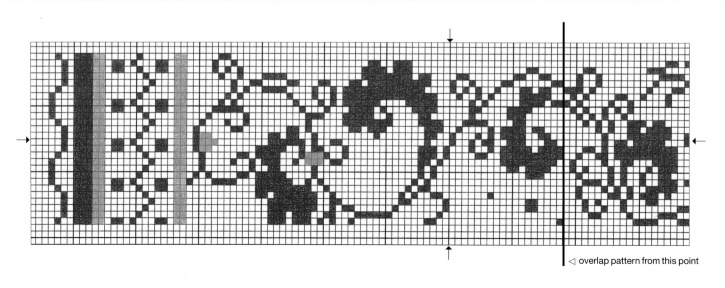

◁ overlap pattern from this point

to work the embroidery

Measure the circumference around the bottom of your chosen lampshade. Cut the Aida band to this length, plus 2cm (¾in) for the centre back seam allowances. Secure the raw edges of the band ends with zigzag stitch.

Start stitching at the centre of the design and in the centre of the Aida band. Repeat the design as many times as needed to fit the length of the band. This may not be an exact number of repeats. To treat the finished embroidery, see page 103.

to make up the lampshade

If the fabric of the shade is not rigid but has a wire rim at the bottom, as shown in the photograph, check for fit and sew up the centre back seam of the embroidered band. Pin and tack the top and bottom edges of the band around the outside of the shade, about 1cm (⅜in) up from the lower edge, then prick stitch or half backstitch it into position by hand.

If there is no wire at the bottom of your chosen shade, sew up the centre back seam and pin and tack the edges of the embroidered band as above, but machine stitch into position.

If the shade is made from a rigid material and there is wire around the bottom, use some fabric adhesive to glue the top and bottom edges of the embroidered band into position on the shade, keeping one end of the seam allowance to the centre back. Lay this flat, and when the other end meets it, fold that end under and lay it on top of the first raw end. Pin down the folded end to secure and slipstitch the two ends together by hand to finish.

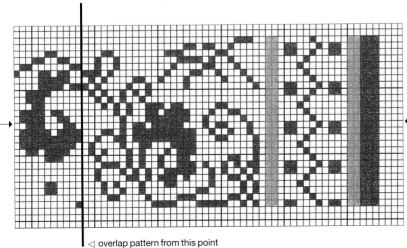

◁ overlap pattern from this point

stranded cottons

DMC	Anchor	Skeins
792	177	3
794	175	3

chapter 1 **the living room**

Toile de Jouy lampshade

This playful see-saw design will amuse adults and children alike. If you wish, you can place the finished shade in a special part of the living room where your children like to relax and read.

measurements

Worked on 16 count Aida, the finished embroidery measures 13 x 7.2cm (5⅛ x 2⅞in). Use 2 strands of cotton in the needle for cross stitch and one strand for backstitch and French knots, working the knots with 2 twists around the needle.

materials

To work the embroidery:
• Lampshade of your choice
• Tracing paper for pattern
• Piece of 16 count white Aida, 5–7.5cm (2–3in) larger all round than lampshade pattern (see below)
• Stranded cotton embroidery threads as specified in the colour key
• Tapestry needle size 24 or 26

To make up the lampshade:
• PVA adhesive or glue gun
• Cotton tape, 1.5cm (⅝in) wide
• White sewing thread
• Basic sewing kit
• Sewing machine

to make the pattern

Place the lampshade at one end of the piece of tracing paper and mark the position of the seam line. Roll the shade right round until the seam is back on the paper again, tracing the top and bottom outlines of the shade as you go. Add 1cm (⅜in) at each end and 2cm (¾in) at the top and bottom of the pattern shape, then cut out. Fold the pattern in half vertically, measure halfway down this fold line and mark in the central position for the embroidery on the pattern.

to work the embroidery

Cut out a piece of white Aida to the appropriate size. As an example, the lampshade used here is 12cm (4¾in) deep; the bottom circumference is 49cm (19¼in) and the top circumference 26cm (10¼in). To allow enough room to fit in the pattern with 5–7.5cm (2–3in) all round, the Aida was cut to 28 x 58.5cm (11 x 23in).

Pin the pattern to the Aida and use a fabric marker to mark the outer edge of the pattern and the positions of the centre lines (1). Unpin the pattern and tack in the centre lines on the Aida to mark the centre position of the embroidery. Start stitching at the centre of the design and at the centre position marked on the Aida. To treat the finished embroidery, see page 103.

to make up the lampshade

Cut out the embroidered fabric into the lampshade shape and secure the raw edges with zigzag stitch. Wrap the fabric around the shade wrong side out, pinning the centre back seam to check the fit. Remove the fabric from the shade, tack and machine stitch down the length of the seam and trim the seam allowance. Turn the embroidered lampshade cover through to the right side, press, and then put it back onto the shade. Apply adhesive to the top and bottom inside edges of the shade. Turn the top and bottom seam allowances to the inside, pressing them down onto the adhesive and snipping into the fabric seam allowance to ensure a snug fit. Use clothes pegs to hold the fabric in place while the adhesive dries. When completely dry, glue on lengths of cotton tape to cover the raw edges of the fabric to neaten.

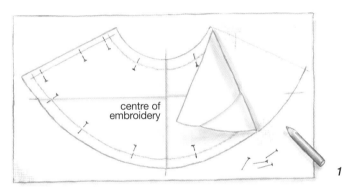

centre of embroidery

1

stranded cottons

	DMC	Anchor	Skeins
	311	148	1
	798	137	1
	793	176	1
	3755	130	1
	775	975	10

French knots

	DMC	Anchor
●	311	148

Backstitch

	DMC	Anchor
▬	311	148

Chinese café curtain

This design was inspired by a modern Chinese trinket pot. I used the separate motifs from the pot and placed them at intervals along the bottom of the café curtain on a background of navy blue fine cotton fabric.

measurements

Worked on 16 count Aida, each finished motif measures 7 x 5cm (2¾ x 2in). Use 2 strands of cotton in the needle throughout, and work French knots with 2 twists around the needle.

materials

To work the embroidery:
• Tracing paper for template
• Piece of 16 count ice-blue Aida to fit as many triangular pieces, each 14 x 19cm (5½ x 7½in), as needed for width of curtain
• Stranded cotton embroidery threads as specified in the colour key
• Tapestry needle size 24 or 26

To make up the curtain:
• Piece of navy blue fine cotton fabric, dimensions as required for size of curtain
• Blue and white sewing threads
• Basic sewing kit
• Sewing machine

to work the embroidery

Trace the triangle template on page 108 and use it to mark out the required number of triangles on the Aida, adding 1cm (⅜in) all round for the seam allowance. Following the template, tack in the centre lines on each triangular piece.

Start stitching at the centre of each design and at the centre position marked on the Aida. To treat the finished embroideries, see page 103.

▷

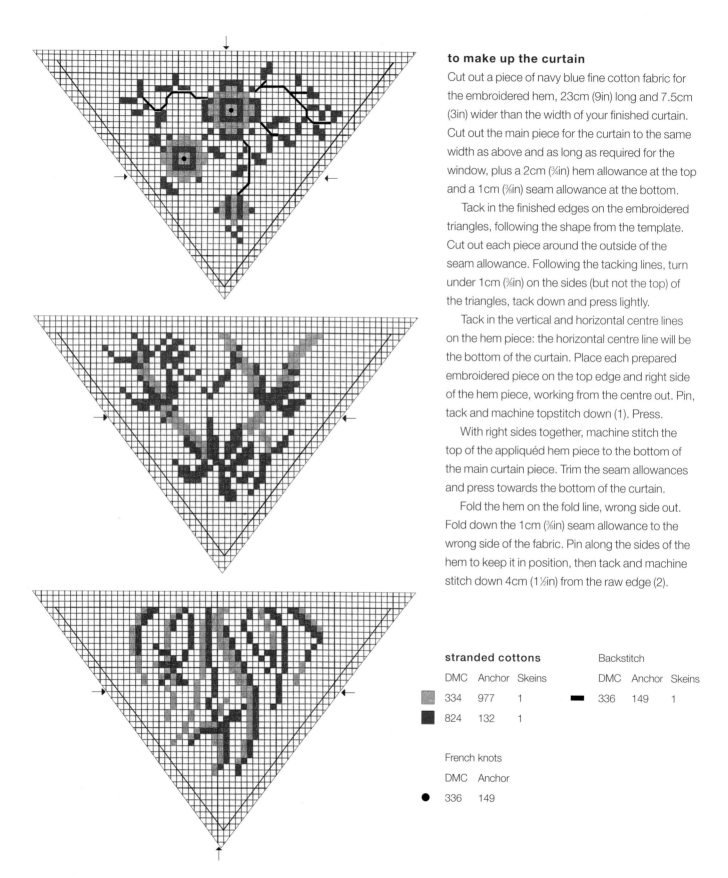

to make up the curtain

Cut out a piece of navy blue fine cotton fabric for the embroidered hem, 23cm (9in) long and 7.5cm (3in) wider than the width of your finished curtain. Cut out the main piece for the curtain to the same width as above and as long as required for the window, plus a 2cm (¾in) hem allowance at the top and a 1cm (⅜in) seam allowance at the bottom.

Tack in the finished edges on the embroidered triangles, following the shape from the template. Cut out each piece around the outside of the seam allowance. Following the tacking lines, turn under 1cm (⅜in) on the sides (but not the top) of the triangles, tack down and press lightly.

Tack in the vertical and horizontal centre lines on the hem piece: the horizontal centre line will be the bottom of the curtain. Place each prepared embroidered piece on the top edge and right side of the hem piece, working from the centre out. Pin, tack and machine topstitch down (1). Press.

With right sides together, machine stitch the top of the appliquéd hem piece to the bottom of the main curtain piece. Trim the seam allowances and press towards the bottom of the curtain.

Fold the hem on the fold line, wrong side out. Fold down the 1cm (⅜in) seam allowance to the wrong side of the fabric. Pin along the sides of the hem to keep it in position, then tack and machine stitch down 4cm (1½in) from the raw edge (2).

stranded cottons

DMC	Anchor	Skeins
334	977	1
824	132	1

Backstitch

DMC	Anchor	Skeins
336	149	1

French knots

DMC	Anchor
● 336	149

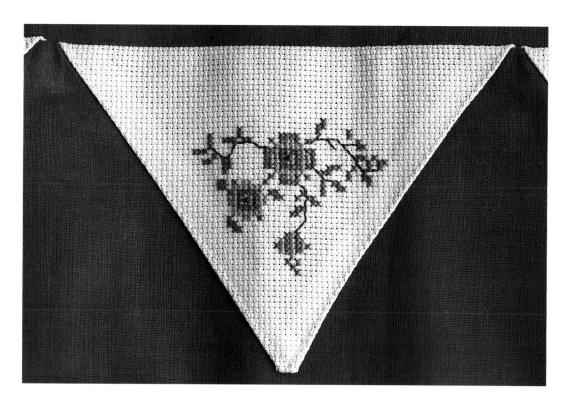

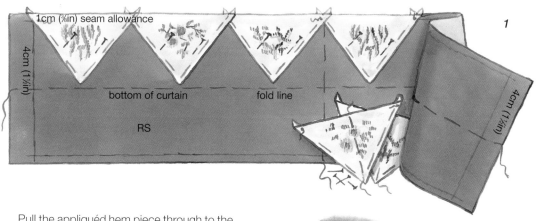

1cm (⅜in) seam allowance

4cm (1½in)

bottom of curtain   fold line

RS

4cm (1½in)

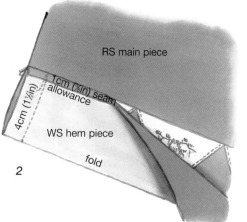

1

Pull the appliquéd hem piece through to the right side and press flat, pressing the fabric on the sides of the curtain at the same time. Pin, tack and slipstitch the hem into position.

Turn in and press 1cm (⅜in) seam allowances along the sides of the main curtain. Pin, tack and slipstitch the side hems by hand.

Fold the top of the curtain hem twice, 1cm (⅜in) at a time, towards the wrong side of the fabric and topstitch down by machine. Finish the top of the curtain according to your choice of rail.

RS main piece

1cm (⅜in) seam allowance

4cm (1½in)

WS hem piece

fold

2

Toile de Jouy bolster cushion

Bolster cushions are simpler to make than you may think and will smarten up any sofa, giving it a look of sophistication and luxury. Embroider this one with a typical Toile de Jouy scene of a young man watching his dog chasing water fowl.

measurements
Worked on 14 count Aida, the finished embroidery measures 26 x 13.7cm (10¼in x 5⅜in). Use 2 strands of cotton in the needle for cross stitch, backstitch on the trees and punt pole, and French knots. Use one strand for backstitch on the man's face and body. Work French knots with 2 twists around the needle.

materials
To work the embroidery:
• Piece of 14 count white Aida, 19cm (7½in) x length of bolster plus 4cm (1½in)
• Stranded cotton embroidery threads as specified in the colour key
• Tapestry needle size 24 or 26

To make up the cushion:
• Bolster cushion of your choice
• Piece of white cotton fabric, dimensions as required for size of cushion (see below)
• White zip, 8–10cm (3–4in) shorter than length of bolster
• Length of piping cord, twice circumference of cushion
• 2 large buttons
• Piece of thin wadding, 10 x 10cm (4 x 4in), to pad buttons (optional)
• White sewing thread
• Basic sewing kit
• Sewing machine

to measure out the fabric
Measure the circumference and length of the bolster cushion. Using a fabric marker, mark out a rectangle to these dimensions on the wrong side of the white cotton fabric, adding a 2cm (¾in) seam allowance all round. Cut out the main cushion cover piece.

Mark and cut out 2 bias strips in cotton fabric (see page 106), each one the length of the circumference of the cushion and wide enough to wrap around the piping cord, adding a 1.5cm (⅝in) seam allowance to each long side of the strip.

Mark and cut out 2 long strips of cotton fabric for each end of the bolster, each 1½ times the circumference measurement and 4cm (1½in) wider than the radius of the ends of the cushion, to give a 2cm (¾in) seam allowance on both long sides of each of the strips.

▷

Cut 2 circles in cotton fabric, each large enough to cover a button, and gather the fabric on the underside. If liked, cut 2 circles in thin wadding, each the same size as the button, to give the buttons a more padded look.

to work the embroidery

Start stitching at the centre of the design and in the centre of the Aida, following the chart. To treat the finished embroidery, see page 103.

to make up the cushion

Place the embroidered Aida centrally along the length of the main cushion cover piece. Turn in 1.5cm (⅝in) along the raw edges of the Aida above and below the embroidery, then pin, tack and machine topstitch down. The raw edges at each side of the embroidered Aida will later be caught in with the piping.

Prepare to insert the zip into the seam by folding the main fabric piece in half lengthways, right sides together. Lay the zip centrally along the length of seam to mark the length of the zip opening. To set in the zip, see page 105.

Cut the piping cord into 2 equal lengths and butt the 2 ends of each piece together to meet, securing with a few hand stitches to keep them in position. Place a bias strip over each piping circle with an overlap of 0.5cm (¼in), placing this over the joined ends of the cord. Wrap, pin and tack the bias strip around the cord and turn under the

overlap pattern from this point ▷

overlapped end of the strip by 0.5cm (¼in), stretching the bias and laying it over the first raw end. Slipstich the two ends together to secure.

Lay the circles of covered piping on the right side and at opposite ends of the main cushion cover piece, raw edges to raw edges. Pin, tack and machine stitch down, using the zipper foot to get as close to the piping as possible (1).

Join the ends of the 2 long fabric strips to make 2 circles. Sew 2 rows of gathering machine stitch on either side of the fabric circles (see Frills, page 107) (2). Gather the bottom edges of the circles to fit the circumference of the bolster cover ends. Gather the top edges of the circles by pulling the threads as tightly as possible to form the centre. This will form 2 circles of gathered fabric for the ends of the cover (3). Knot the threads to secure.

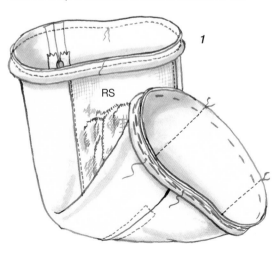

1

RS

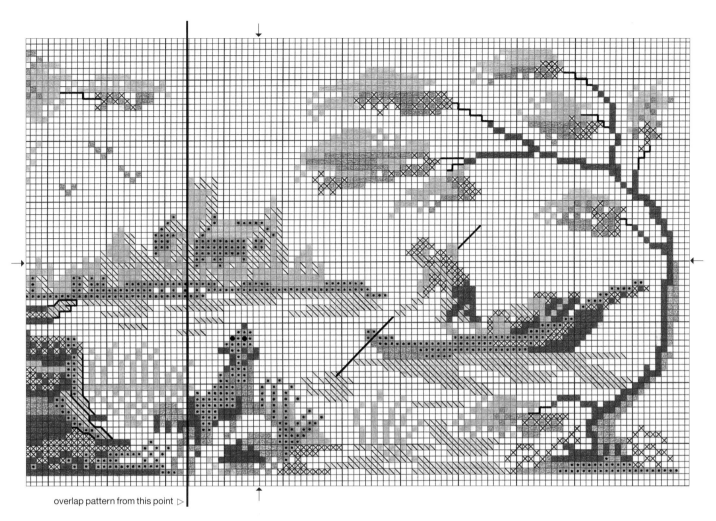

overlap pattern from this point ▷

2

3

Unzip the main cushion cover piece and pull through to the wrong side. With right sides together, pin and tack the two gathered end pieces to the ends of the main piece. Machine stitch using the zipper foot to get as close to the piping as possible. Trim the seam allowances, turn through to the right side and insert the bolster. Close the zip. Hand sew a row of running stitches around the edges of the 2 button fabric circles. If liked, place wadding in the centre of the wrong side of the fabric. Place a button in the centre of each fabric circle, on top of the wadding if used, and gather up the fabric to the underside of the button. Secure with a few hand stitches. Hand stitch a covered button onto each end of the bolster, covering the centre gathers.

stranded cottons

	DMC	Anchor	Skeins
■	3750	1036	2
⊠	824	143	2
·	3760	161	2
▨	813	130	2
◨	3761	928	2
▦	825	142	2

French knots

	DMC	Anchor
●	3750	1036

Backstitch

	DMC	Anchor
▬	3750	1036

Portuguese tablecloth

Decorative Portuguese glazed tiles are known as *azulejo*, a Moorish word meaning 'smooth'. The design on this tablecloth was inspired by two such tiles, discovered by my father in the Algarve area of the country.

measurements

Worked on 14 count Aida, the finished centrepiece embroidery measures 12.3 x 12.3cm (4⅞ x 4⅞in) and the corner pieces 7.5 x 7.5cm (3 x 3in). Use 2 strands of cotton in the needle throughout.

materials

To work the embroidery:
• 2 pieces of 14 count antique white Aida, 25 x 25cm (9⅞ x 9⅞in) for centre and 30 x 30cm (12 x 12in) for corners
• Stranded cotton embroidery threads as specified in the colour key
• Tapestry needle size 24 or 26
To make up the tablecloth:
• Piece of navy blue cotton fabric, 66 x 66cm (26 x 26in)
• Navy blue and cream sewing threads
• Basic sewing kit
• Sewing machine

to work the embroidery

For the centrepiece embroidery, start stitching at the centre of the design and in the centre of the Aida, following the chart.

For the 4 corner embroideries, tack in the right-angled corner shapes, leaving a margin of 4–5cm (1½–2in) all round. From each corner point, tack in the diagonal line (1). Start stitching from the corner of the design and at the corner point marked on the Aida. To treat the finished embroideries, see page 103.

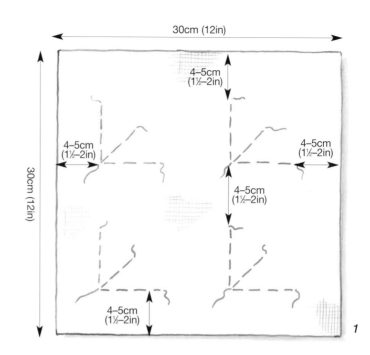

1

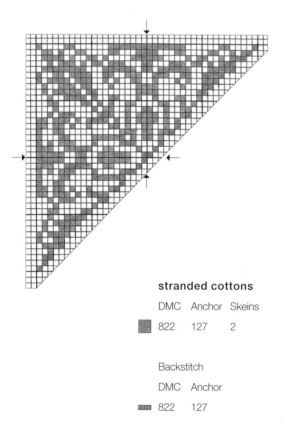

stranded cottons

	DMC	Anchor	Skeins
	822	127	2

Backstitch

	DMC	Anchor
	822	127

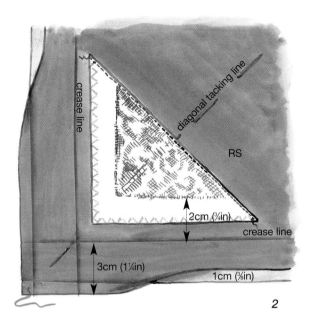

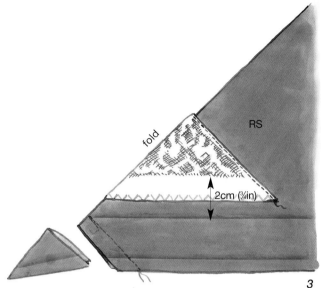

2

3

to make up the tablecloth

On the right side of the navy blue cotton fabric, tack in the vertical and horizontal centre lines, plus the diagonals.

Mark the hem fold line 3cm (1¼in) in from the edge of the fabric using tailor's chalk. Fold the hem to the right side of the fabric and press to make a crease line on the hem position. Open out the fabric, then press in a 1cm (⅜in) seam allowance all round. Open out the fabric again.

Prepare the finished embroideries by cutting off the surplus Aida, leaving a margin of 1.5cm (⅝in) all round each piece. Secure the raw edges with zigzag stitch. For the centrepiece, turn the edges under by 1cm (⅜in) and tack down. For the 4 corner pieces, fold back the long edge only, leaving about 0.3cm (⅛in) free between the fold and the embroidery, and tack down. Cut off the surplus fabric that sticks out at the corners.

Place an embroidered corner piece in each corner of the tablecloth, with the raw edges towards the crease line of the hem and positioned so that the hem does not cover the embroidery when folded over. Pin, tack and machine topstitch down (2). Place the embroidered centrepiece in the centre of the tablecloth, with the corners placed on the vertical and horizontal centre lines

(not on the diagonals). Pin, tack and machine topstitch down.

The corners of the tablecloth are mitred. At each corner, fold in the corner point to the diagonal tacking line of the tablecloth and crease to mark the seam line. Open out the corner and then fold it in half along the diagonal tacking line of the tablecloth, right side out. Machine stitch through both thicknesses of fabric along the seam line, then cut off the surplus fabric leaving a 1cm (⅜in) seam allowance (3). Turn the mitred corner to the right side and press. Check that the mitred corner fits and lies flat.

When all 4 corners have been mitred, turn the 1cm (⅜in) seam allowance to the inside of the hem. Pin, tack and machine topstitch the hem into position (4). Press to neaten.

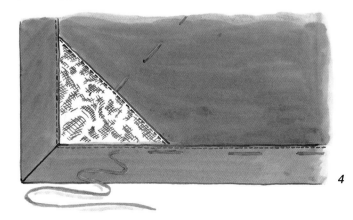

4

The kitchen

The kitchen plays host to a lot of activity and is the hub of the household, so this is a room that should look cheerful, light and sunny. As it is also a practical space, the lively blue and white designs in this chapter fulfil both decorative and useful functions. Nothing could be more practical than a pot holder with which to handle hot pans while cooking, but in this case it also sports an eye-catching Dutch Delft motif. For the table, there is a choice of napkin designs, plus napkin rings, a Chinese-style coaster and a coffee pot warmer that will make an unusual talking point when the family is relaxing at the end of a special meal.

The designs can, of course, be adapted to other items: use the pot holder motif in the centre of a set of cushions for kitchen chairs, turn the coffee pot warmer design into a framed picture, or embroider the napkin motifs onto a pretty hand towel. Decorating your kitchen with real Delft tiles would add the finishing touch.

Wedgwood napkins

These fresh white napkins embroidered with Wedgwood motifs would add the perfect finishing touch to a table laid for a celebration meal. Repeat the designs for as many napkins as you like and perhaps add it to a matching tablecloth.

measurements

Worked on 14 count Aida, the finished boat design measures 11 x 9.5cm (4⅜ x 3¾in) and the building and willow tree design 9 x 7.5cm (3½ x 3in). Use 2 strands of cotton in the needle for cross stitch and one strand for backstitch and French knots. Work French knots with 2 twists around the needle.

materials

To work the embroidery:
- 2 pieces of white cotton fabric, each 55 x 55cm (21¾ x 21¾in)
- 2 pieces of 14 count white Aida, each 21 x 21cm (8¼ x 8¼in)
- Stranded cotton embroidery threads as specified in the colour key
- Tapestry needle size 24 or 26

To make up the napkins:
- White sewing thread
- Basic sewing kit
- Sewing machine

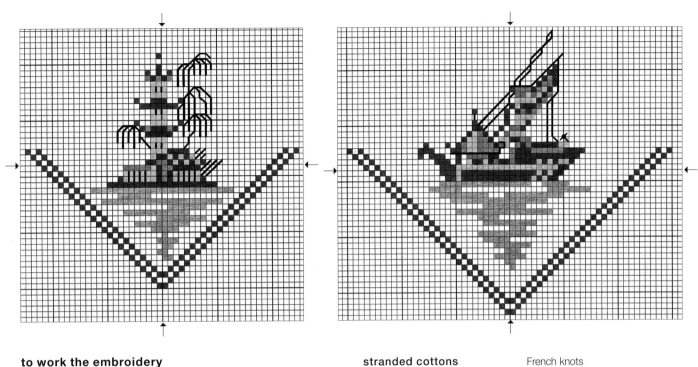

to work the embroidery

Start stitching at the centre of the design and in the centre of the Aida, following the chart. To treat the finished embroidery, see page 103.

to make up the napkins

Cut away excess fabric from around each embroidery, leaving 2cm (¾in) at the bottom of the design and 1.5cm (⅝in) at the top. Fold this 1.5cm (⅝in) seam allowance to the wrong side along the 2 top edges and tack down (1).

Fold in the hem and seam allowances on each piece of white cotton fabric in the same way as for the Portuguese Tablecloth on page 30. Tack in one diagonal, then follow the tablecloth instructions for positioning and stitching down the embroidery, mitring the corners and finishing the hem.

stranded cottons

	DMC	Anchor	Skeins
■	336	149	1
▨	824	147	1
▨	519	1038	1
▨	826	146	1

French knots

	DMC	Anchor	Skeins
●	939	152	1

Backstitch

	DMC	Anchor
▬	939	152

1

fold

1.5cm (⅝in)

2cm (¾in)

Simple napkin ring

This simple design was taken from a plate and can be repeated on several napkin rings to make a set. To add variety to the collection, reverse the colours on some of the rings by sewing white cross stitch on a navy blue background.

measurements

Worked on 14 count Aida, the finished embroidery measures 15.5 x 4.2cm (6⅛ x 1⅝in). Use 2 strands of cotton in the needle throughout.

materials

To work the embroidery:
• Piece of 14 count antique white Aida, 26 x 16cm (10¼ x 6¼in)
• Stranded cotton embroidery threads as specified in the colour key
• Tapestry needle size 24 or 26

To make up the napkin ring:
• Piece of medium-weight interlining, 18.2 x 13.2cm (7⅛ x 5¼in)
• White cotton sewing thread
• Basic sewing kit

to work the embroidery

Start stitching at the centre of the design and in the centre of the Aida, following the chart. To treat the finished embroidery, see page 103.

to make up the napkin ring

Cut off the excess Aida, leaving 4.5cm (1¾in) on the long sides of the embroidery and 1.3cm (½in) at the ends: this allows for 1.3cm (½in) seam allowances all round.

Pin, tack and machine stitch the interlining to the wrong side of the embroidered Aida around the edges and press flat. Place the two long edges right sides together and pin, tack and machine stitch the seam.

Use a piece of wooden dowelling or similar to help push the Aida through to the right side. Place the seam in the centre back of the embroidery and press flat.

Turn the raw ends of the fabric to the inside and tack down on the edges of the embroidery. Slipstitch the two ends together, making the sewing as invisible as possible, to form the napkin ring. To press, roll up a towel and place it inside the ring. Press gently, covering the embroidery with a cloth to protect the stitches.

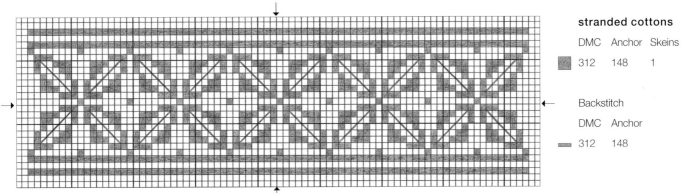

stranded cottons

DMC	Anchor	Skeins
312	148	1

Backstitch

DMC	Anchor
312	148

Pictorial coffee pot warmer

This charming grazing rabbit design was taken from a mug made in the 18th century. The rabbits are nibbling grass among spring flowers, beneath a large tree with fungus growing from its bark. This pretty embroidery would make an unusual Easter present.

measurements
Worked on 16 count Aida, the finished embroidery measures 16.5 x 14.5cm (6½ x 5¾in). Use 2 strands of cotton in the needle throughout.

materials
To work the embroidery:
• **Piece of 16 count ice-blue Aida (see opposite)**
• **Stranded cotton embroidery threads as specified in the colour key**
• **Tapestry needle size 24 or 26**
To make up the coffee pot warmer:
• **Piece of navy blue cotton fabric, 5 x 10cm (2 x 4in), for button loops**
• **Piece of navy blue cotton fabric, same size as Aida**
• **Piece of medium wadding, same size as Aida**
• **2 buttons**
• **White and navy blue sewing threads**
• **Basic sewing kit**
• **Sewing machine**

to work the embroidery
For a standard-sized coffee pot, cut out a piece of Aida 38 x 20cm (15 x 8in). Adjust the measurements as necessary for a larger pot, allowing a 1.5cm (⅝in) seam allowance all round (see below). Start stitching at the centre of the design and in the centre of the Aida, following the chart. Treat the finished embroidery (see page 103).

to make up the warmer
Measure the coffee pot from just under the pouring lip to the base, and then around the circumference at the middle. Mark these two dimensions on the embroidered Aida with a fabric marker or tacking, in such a way that the embroidery is in the correct centred position. Allowing 1.5cm (⅝in) extra all round for seam allowances, cut out the embroidered Aida to the measured size.

Cut 2 strips, each 2.5 x 10cm (1 x 4in), from navy blue cotton fabric for the button loops and follow the method for making ties on page 106.

Tack the wadding to the wrong side of the navy blue cotton fabric. Pin and tack the padded cotton and the embroidered Aida right sides together and machine stitch along the top seam. Turn the joined pieces right sides out and machine topstitch the seam allowances down towards the back (navy blue cotton side) of the warmer, 0.3cm (⅛in) away from the seam. Trim the seam allowance.

Mark the button loop positions on the right side of the embroidered piece inside the coffee pot handle position, measuring 6.5cm (2⅝in) from the centre of one button loop to the centre of the other. Pin, tack and machine stitch the button

▷

loops into position (1).

Place the right sides of the front and back pieces together and pin, tack and machine stitch the side seams. Trim the excess seam allowances. Pin, tack and machine stitch along the bottom edge, leaving a gap of about 8cm (3in). Trim the excess seam allowance and pull the warmer to the right side through the gap. Turn in the raw edges of the gap and pin, tack and slipstitch together by hand.

Mark the positions of the buttons and stitch them on. Press lightly to neaten.

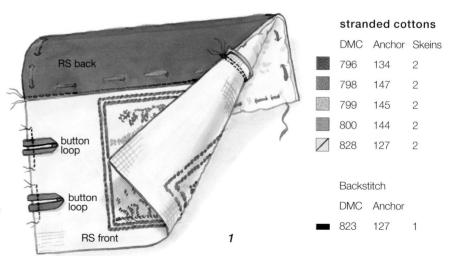

1

stranded cottons

DMC	Anchor	Skeins
796	134	2
798	147	2
799	145	2
800	144	2
828	127	2

Backstitch

DMC	Anchor	
823	127	1

Dutch Delft pot holder

The design for this pot holder was taken from a tall Dutch Delft liquor jar, which belongs to my family and through their connection with shipping was brought to England from Holland. The design on the jar shows a large stylized flower surrounded by foliage, and the floral motif is repeated in a border at the top and around the base of the jar. The pot holder is bound with bias cut strips of navy blue and white gingham, continuing the blue and white theme and making a decorative but practical finish.

▷

measurements

Worked on 14 count Aida, the finished embroidery measures 11.5 x 11.5cm (4½ x 4½in). Use 2 strands of cotton in the needle throughout.

materials

To work the embroidery:
• Tracing paper for template
• Piece of 14 count white Aida, 20 x 20cm (8 x 8in)
• Stranded cotton embroidery threads as specified in the colour key
• Tapestry needle size 24 or 26
To make up the pot holder:
• Piece of medium-weight cotton wadding, 16.5 x 16.5cm (6½ x 6½in)
• Piece of navy blue and white small-squared cotton gingham, 59 x 59cm (23 x 23in)
• White sewing thread
• Basic sewing kit
• Sewing machine

to work the embroidery

Start stitching at the centre of the design and in the centre of the Aida, following the chart. To treat the finished embroidery, see page 103.

to make up the pot holder

Cut out a pattern 16.5 x 16.5cm (6½ x 6½in) for the pot holder from tracing paper. Mark in the centre lines and 1cm (⅜in) seam allowances all round. Tack in the centre lines on the embroidered Aida and place the tracing paper pattern on the fabric, matching the centre lines. Pin the pattern in position and cut the Aida to shape.

Pin and tack the cotton wadding to the wrong side of the Aida. Cut out a piece of cotton gingham to the same size as the Aida and wadding, then pin and tack it to the wadded side of the Aida, wrong sides together. The wadding will be sandwiched between the Aida and the gingham. Machine stitch all three layers together.

Cut bias strips from the gingham fabric to make a length of bias tape 76 x 5cm (30 x 2in), following the instructions on page 106.

Cut out a strip of gingham 18 x 3.5cm (7 x 1⅜in) and make up into a hanging loop following the instructions on page 106. Fold the loop in half,

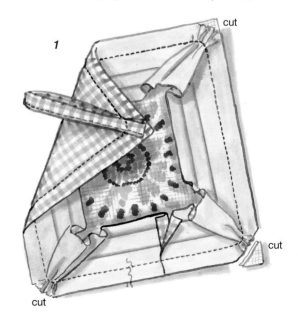

1

cut

cut

cut

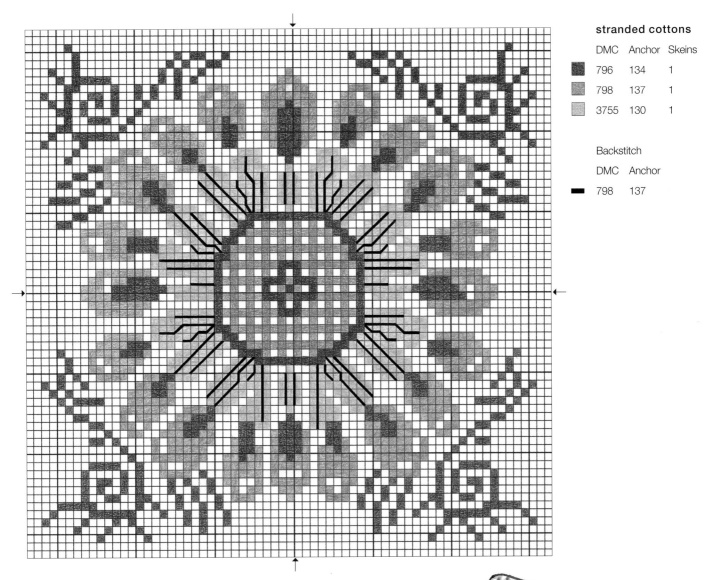

stranded cottons

DMC	Anchor	Skeins
796	134	1
798	137	1
3755	130	1

Backstitch

DMC	Anchor
798	137

then pin and tack it to the back (gingham side) of the pot holder at one of the corners, matching raw edges to raw edges.

Starting from just beyond one corner and with 1cm seam allowance, fold back one end of the bias tape back onto itself and to the wrong side. Pin the tape onto the front of the pot holder right sides together. Tack and machine stitch the bias tape into position, rounding each corner slightly as you go. This will make it easier to turn the tape over to the back of the pot holder. Trim the corners of the pot holder (1).

Turn the bias tape to the back of the pot holder,

folding the raw edge under by 1cm (⅜in), then pin, tack and slipstitch the bias hem and folded join to secure (2). Turn in the raw edge of the end of the bias tape and stitch. Press lightly from the back of the pot holder to neaten.

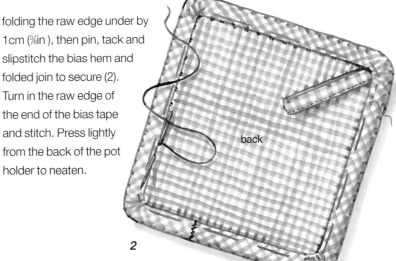

2

Ming coaster

A blue and white Chinese plate dating from the 15th-century Yongle Ming period inspired the design for this large coaster. The pattern on the plate is dripping with plump ripe grapes, making it a highly appropriate design for a coaster with a sparkling glass of wine placed on it.

measurements
Worked on 16 count Aida, the finished embroidery measures 8.5 x 8.5cm (3⅜ x 3⅜in). Use 2 strands of cotton in the needle throughout, and work French knots with 2 twists around the needle.

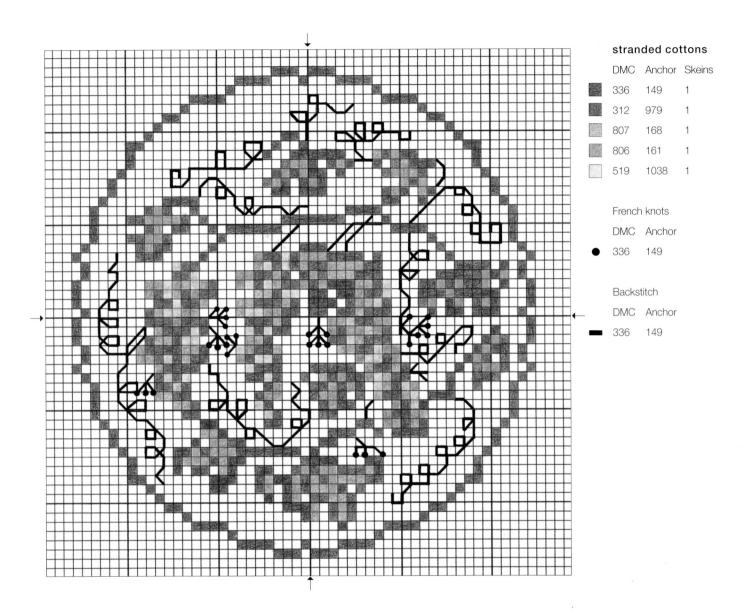

stranded cottons

DMC	Anchor	Skeins
336	149	1
312	979	1
807	168	1
806	161	1
519	1038	1

French knots

DMC	Anchor
336	149

Backstitch

DMC	Anchor
336	149

materials

To work the embroidery:
- Piece of 16 count ice-blue Aida, 20 x 20cm (8 x 8in)
- Stranded cotton embroidery threads as specified in the colour key
- Tapestry needle size 24 or 26

To make up the coaster:
- Piece of iron-on medium-weight interfacing, 10 x 10cm (4 x 4in)
- Glass coaster to take embroidery, outside diameter 9.5cm (3¾in)
- Basic sewing kit

to work the embroidery

Start stitching at the centre of the design and in the centre of the Aida, following the chart. To treat the finished embroidery, see page 103.

to make up the coaster

Back the embroidered Aida with iron-on interfacing to prevent the edge of the fabric from fraying when you cut it to shape.

Follow the manufacturer's instructions for placing the embroidery inside the glass coaster.

The bathroom

A light and airy bathroom lifts the spirits and clears the mind after a long, hard day, and the embroideries in this chapter are designed to enhance this calming ambience.

Relax in a hot bath scented with lavender oils, letting the herbal aroma drift with your thoughts. Then step out onto a pretty bathmat decorated with an unusual Delft-inspired shoe design, feeling the soft towelling between your toes, and dry your body with a white Willow Pattern towel.

Next, place your work-worn clothes in the generous-sized Toile de Jouy linen bag ready for the next day's wash, then rub soothing oils into your skin and remove any excess with a tissue pulled from an intricately embroidered tissue box. Do you feel better now?

To ring the changes, stitch a pair of shoes from the bathmat motif to frame as a bathroom picture, or add the Willow Pattern design to a white or navy blue bathrobe to match the towels. The intricate cottonwool bag design would be perfect for the lid of a trinket box or embroidered onto a sachet filled with lavender pot pourri.

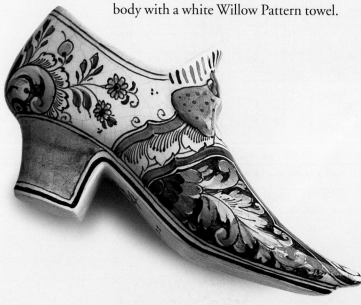

Tissue-box cover

The decorative birds and flowers depicted in the intricate design on this tissue-box cover were inspired by an ornate blue and white Islamic Safavid plate, made in the late 17th century.

- Piece of thick wadding, 30.5 x 18cm (12 x 7in)
- Superglue
- 36cm (14in) length of white bias tape, 5cm (2in) wide
- Piece of iron-on fusion webbing, 16 x 9cm (6¼ x 3½in)
- Double-sided adhesive tape, 5cm (2in) wide
- A4 sheet of white paper
- 114cm (45in) length of cord, to match paint colour
- Basic sewing kit
- Sewing machine

measurements
Worked on 16 count Aida, the finished embroidery measures 23 x 13.8cm (9 x 5⅜in). Use 2 strands of cotton in the needle for cross stitch and one strand for backstitch.

materials
To work the embroidery:
- Piece of 16 count ice-blue Aida, 36 x 25.5cm (14 x 10in)
- Stranded cotton embroidery threads as specified in the colour key
- Tapestry needle size 24 or 26
To make up the tissue-box cover:
- Unpainted wooden tissue-box cover
- Dark blue acrylic permanent paint, to match DMC stranded cotton 312/Anchor 979
- 2.5cm (1in) bristle paintbrush

to work the embroidery
Start stitching at the centre of the design and in the centre of the Aida, following the chart. To treat the finished embroidery, see page 103.

to make up the tissue-box cover
Paint the wooden tissue-box cover with two coats of dark blue acrylic permanent paint.

Cut the wadding to fit the tissue-box top exactly. Glue the wadding onto the top of the box using superglue and cut it away where it covers the hole for the tissues to come through.

Following the manufacturer's instructions, lay the piece of iron-on fusion webbing onto the wrong side of the embroidered Aida, placing it on the area corresponding to where the hole in the box will be. Iron on the fusion webbing and peel off the backing paper. The remaining sticky surface on the fabric

▷

overlap pattern from this point ▷

prevents the Aida from fraying when the hole for the tissues is cut.

Cut out the Aida around the area that corresponds to the inside of the hole, leaving a 1cm (⅜in) seam allowance. Snip into the curved ends of the seam allowance and turn it back to the wrong side of the embroidery. The snipped fabric at the ends will help in turning the facing back on itself. Using some of the fusion webbing paper that has been peeled off, and laying sticky side of paper to sticky side of fabric, iron down the seam

allowance of the hole, easing out the snipped area at the curved ends of the opening.

Measure the circumference of the box hole and cut the bias tape for the facing 3cm (1⅛in) longer to allow for turning the ends. Machine a loose line of stitching along one long edge of the bias facing. Help to ease the facing around the curved corners of the hole by pulling one of the threads to gather it slightly. Fold in one end by 1.5cm (⅝in) to the wrong side of the facing, then fold in 0.5cm (¼in) along the length of the facing towards the wrong side (1).

stranded cottons

	DMC	Anchor	Skeins
■	312	979	2
■	517	146	2
◩	334	145	1
▨	827	976	2

Backstitch

	DMC	Anchor
▬	312	979

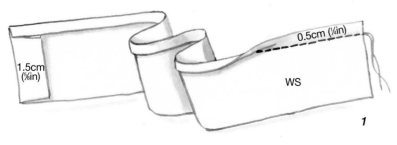

1.5cm (⅝in)

0.5cm (¼in)

WS

1

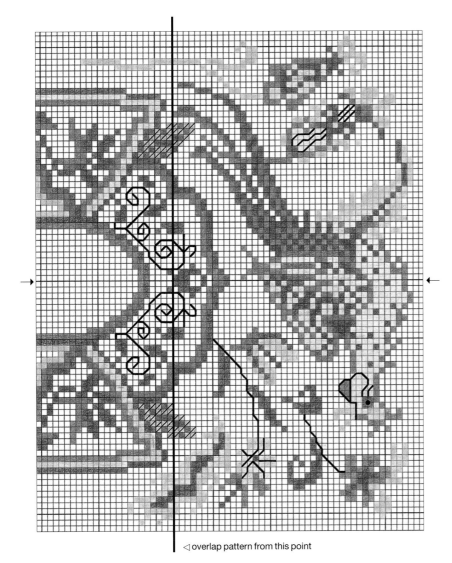

◁ overlap pattern from this point

Starting with the unfolded end of the facing, place the folded edge to the folded edge of the hole in the Aida, wrong sides together. Pin the bias facing to the Aida to keep it in position, ending with the folded end overlapping the raw end. Slipstitch by hand to secure the folded end to the raw end and stitch the bias facing and Aida together around the circumference of the hole.

Measure 4cm (1½in) down from the flower on the outside edge of the embroidery and cut away the excess Aida evenly around the outside edge. Secure the raw edges with zigzag stitch.

Cut pieces of double-sided adhesive tape and stick them inside the tissue box around the hole. Pin the embroidered Aida to the wadding on top of the box, right side up. Push the bias facing through to the inside of the box and snip into the facing at the curved ends of the hole. Peel off the

paper backing from the adhesive tape and stick down the bias facing. You can lift it on and off the adhesive tape until the hole in the Aida is in the correct position. Superglue down for extra strength.

Cut strips of double-sided adhesive tape about 2cm (¾in) wide and stick them around the top edge of the sides of the tissue box, making sure they do not show below the fabric. Remove the pins from the Aida and manoeuvre the embroidery into the correct position, sticking down the two long sides of Aida fabric to the edge of the box. Repeat for the two short ends, making an angled fold for each corner (2). Pin down the angled corners to keep them in position and then glue them down, adding superglue around the edges of the fabric as well. Be careful not to glue the pins, as they will be difficult to remove.

Cut a piece of white paper to the inside measurements of the top of the tissue box. Stick pieces of double-sided adhesive tape to the inside of the top of the box, place the piece of paper inside and stick down to neaten. Carefully cut the paper away from the hole.

Find the centre of the length of cord and mark it with a pin. Start gluing the cord from the centre of one of the short ends of the box, making sure you cover the raw fabric edge. Carry on gluing both sides until you reach the opposite end, leaving a gap of about 5cm (2in). Tie the two ends of the cord into a knot and glue the knot down to keep it in place. Knot the free ends of the cord to an appropriate length and cut off below this.

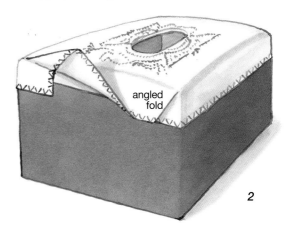

angled fold

2

chapter 3 **the bathroom**

Toile de Jouy linen bag

Imagine washing your clothes in a stream on a sunny day. This design for a linen bag depicts a typically romantic style of Toile de Jouy – and makes washing look a pleasure!

measurements
Worked on 14 count Aida, the finished embroidery measures 19.3 x 18cm (7⅝ x 7in). Use 2 strands of cotton in the needle for cross stitch and one strand for backstitch.

materials
To work the embroidery:
• Piece of 14 count antique white Aida, 30.5 x 30.5cm (12 x 12in)
• Stranded cotton embroidery threads as specified in the colour key
• Tapestry needle size 24 or 26
To make up the linen bag:
• Tracing paper for pattern
• 1.5m (1⅝yd) navy blue strong cotton fabric, 114cm (45in) wide
• Piece of medium-weight interfacing, 12.5 x 6.5cm (5 x 2⅝in)
• Navy blue and white sewing threads
• Basic sewing kit
• Sewing machine

stranded cottons			stranded cottons			Backstitch	
DMC	Anchor	Skeins	DMC	Anchor	Skeins	DMC	Anchor
336	149	2	3755	130	2	825	142
825	142	2	3753	1031	2		
334	145	2	644	830	2		

to work the embroidery

Start stitching at the centre of the design and in the centre of the Aida, following the chart. To treat the finished embroidery, see page 103.

to make up the bag

CUTTING OUT

Following the pattern diagram, make tracing paper patterns for the main bag piece and the pocket. Pin the pattern for the main bag piece to the navy blue cotton fabric and cut out. Mark the buttonholes and pocket position with tailor's chalk before unpinning the pattern.

Pin the pocket pattern to the navy blue fabric and cut out 2 pocket pieces. Mark in the embroidery position on one of the pieces, before unpinning the pattern.

Cut out a strip of navy blue fabric for the hanging loop measuring 23 x 7cm (9 x 2¾in).

Cut out 2 strips of navy blue fabric for the tie, each measuring 84 x 6cm (33 x 2⅜in).

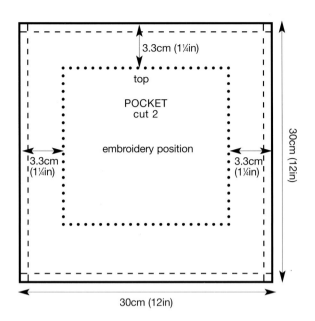

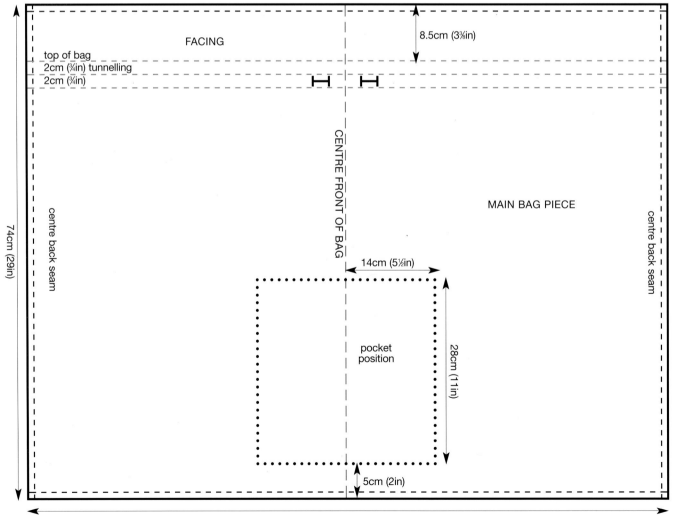

POCKET

On the right side of one of the pocket pieces, tack in the vertical and horizontal centre lines in contrasting thread.

Trim away excess fabric around the embroidery on the Aida, leaving about 2cm (¾in) from the edge of the embroidery all round. Secure the raw edges with zigzag stitch. Tack in the centre lines with contrasting thread.

Turn back and tack the edges of the Aida to the underside, about 4 squares away from the edge of the embroidery. Appliqué the embroidery right side up to the right side of the prepared pocket piece, matching the tacking lines and placing the design onto the chalk marks for the correct position. Pin, tack and machine topstitch down with white sewing thread.

Place the second pocket piece onto the appliquéd pocket piece, right sides together. Pin, tack and machine stitch with navy blue thread and a 1cm (⅜in) seam allowance, but leave a little gap at the bottom edge of the pocket. Pull the pocket through to the right side and neatly press then slipstitch the gap closed.

TIE AND HANGING LOOP

Make the hanging loop by following the instructions on page 106. Then pin, tack and machine topstitch along the open edge, making a strip measuring 23 x 2cm (9 x ¾in).

Pin, tack and machine stitch together the 2 strips that make the tie to make one long strip. Make up the tie, using the same method as for the hanging loop.

Fold the loop piece in half. Pin the loop onto the right side of the main bag piece, the looped end towards the centre of the bag, raw edges to centre back seam and 10cm (4in) down from the line that will be the top of the bag. Place the loop at a slight upwards angle to make it easier to hang on a hook. Tack and machine stitch to secure.

ASSEMBLY

Pin, tack and machine topstitch the pocket into position on the centre front of the bag with navy blue thread, using the tailor's chalk marks as a guide to correct placing.

Place the interfacing at the back of the buttonhole markings, on the wrong side of the fabric. Pin and tack down. Make the buttonholes, stitching them from the right side of the fabric (see page 105).

Pin, tack and machine stitch the centre back seam of the bag, wrong side out. Open out the seam, press, and pin the bottom of the seam to the bottom centre front of the bag, right sides together. Pin, tack and machine stitch along the bottom of the bag to close (1). Trim the excess seam allowance and turn to the right side. Press.

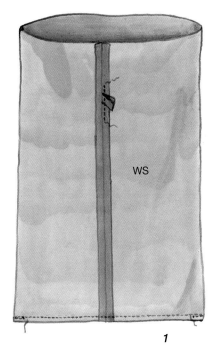

1

FINISHING

Turn in the top raw edge of the bag to the wrong side by 1cm (⅜in) and machine topstitch down. Turn the facing to the inside of the bag by 7.5cm (3in). Pin, tack and press into position.

Machine stitch 2 lines, 2cm (¾in) apart, on either side of the buttonholes as marked. This will catch down the facing as you sew, thereby forming the tunnelling (2).

Thread the tie through a buttonhole, pushing it through the tunnelling until it comes out of the other buttonhole (see page 106), and knot each end to secure. Snip the raw ends to neaten.

2

Dutch Delft cottonwool bag

Some of my family work in shipping and many souvenirs have been brought home from different parts of the world. The design on this cottonwool bag has been taken from one such item, a pretty Dutch Delft trinket box.

measurements
Worked on 16 count Aida, the finished embroidery measures 14.5 x 13.5cm (5¾ x 5¼in). Use 2 strands of cotton in the needle for cross stitch and one strand for French knots with 2 twists around the needle.

materials
To work the embroidery:
• Piece of 16 count ice-blue Aida, 25.5 x 25.5cm (10 x 10in)
• Stranded cotton embroidery threads as specified in the colour key
• Tapestry needle size 24 or 26
To make up the bag:
• Piece of navy blue cotton fabric, 122 x 30.5cm (49 x 12in)
• Piece of medium-weight interfacing, 10 x 5cm (4 x 2in)
• Paper for pattern
• 84cm (33in) length of blue cord
• Navy blue and white sewing threads
• Basic sewing kit
• Sewing machine

to work the embroidery
Start stitching at the centre of the design and in the centre of the Aida, following the chart. To treat the finished embroidery, see page 103.

▷

stranded cottons

DMC	Anchor	Skeins
791	178	1
792	177	1
3807	176	1
794	175	1
827	159	1

French knots

DMC	Anchor
791	178

to make up the bag

CUTTING OUT

Following the pattern diagram, make a tracing paper pattern for the main bag piece. Pin the pattern to the navy blue cotton fabric and cut out on the fold. Mark the buttonholes and pocket position with tailor's chalk before unpinning the pattern.

Make a tracing paper pattern for the pocket lining measuring 17 x 17cm (6¾ x 6¾in). Pin the pattern to the navy blue fabric and cut out the pocket lining.

POCKET

Tack in the horizontal and vertical centre lines on the pocket lining and the embroidered Aida. Place the pieces right sides together, matching the tacking lines, and trim the Aida to the same size as the pocket lining. Pin, tack and machine stitch the two pieces together with a 1.5cm (⅝in) seam allowance, leaving a 5cm (2in) gap at the bottom of the pocket. Trim the seam allowances and pull the pocket through to the right side. Slipstitch the gap closed by hand. Press the pocket from the lining side to neaten.

Pin and tack the pocket into position on the centre front of the bag, using the chalk marks as a guide to correct placing. Machine topstitch into position with white sewing thread, about 0.3cm (⅛in) in from the edge of the embroidered pocket.

BUTTONHOLES

Place the interfacing behind the buttonhole markings, on the wrong side of the fabric. Pin and tack down. Make the buttonholes, stitching from the right side of the fabric (see page 105).

ASSEMBLY

Fold the bag in half, wrong side out, placing the short ends together to make the top. Pin, tack and machine stitch the side seams. Trim the seam allowances and secure the raw edges with zigzag stitch. Turn the bag to the right side. Press gently to neaten.

FINISHING

Turn in the top raw edge of the bag to the wrong side by 1cm (⅜in). Pin, tack and machine topstitch down. Turn the facing towards the inside of the bag, positioning the bottom edge 1cm (⅜in) below the buttonholes. Pin and tack down.

Machine stitch 2 lines, 2cm (¾in) apart, on either side of the buttonholes as marked. This will catch down the facing as you go, thereby forming the tunnelling (the principle is shown in illustration (2) on page 57). Thread one end of the blue cord through a buttonhole (see page 106), feeding the cord through the tunnelling so that it comes out through the other buttonhole. (Make sure that the other end of the cord does not get lost inside the tunnelling.) Cut the ends of the cord to a suitable length and tie into knots to prevent fraying. Pull and tie the cord ends to close the bag.

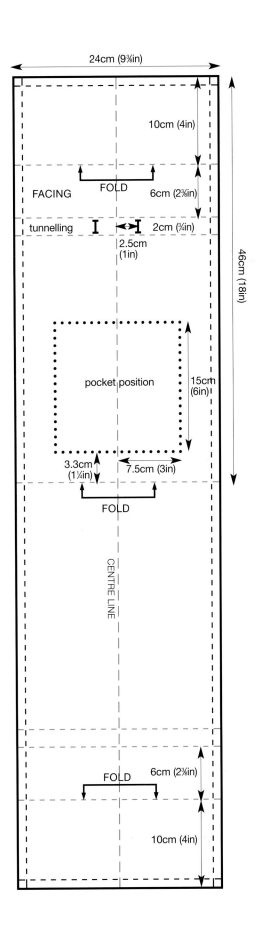

Willow Pattern hand towels

These two hand towels with their pretty Willow Pattern designs would look fresh in any blue and white bathroom. You can adapt the designs by either repeating or shortening the patterns for different-sized towels to add to your bathroom collection.

measurements

Worked on an Aida band (see below), the finished embroidery measures 38.5 x 4.7cm (15¼ x 1⅞in) for the white towel and 37 x 4cm (14⅝ x ½in) for the blue towel. Use 2 strands of cotton in the needle throughout and work French knots with 2 twists around the needle.

materials

To work the embroidery:
- 2 Aida bands with dark blue edging, 6cm (2⅜in) wide with 28 stitches across width x 55cm (21¾in) long
- Stranded cotton embroidery threads as specified in the colour key
- Tapestry needle size 24 or 26

To make up the towels:
- 1 blue and 1 white hand towel, each 90 x 50.5cm (36 x 20in)
- Blue and white sewing threads to match towels
- Basic sewing kit
- Sewing machine

to work the embroidery

Start stitching at the centre of the design and in the centre of the Aida, following the chart. To treat the finished embroidery, see page 103.

to make up the hand towels

Find the centre of the embroidered Aida band and of the width of the towel. Mark both centres with a   ▷

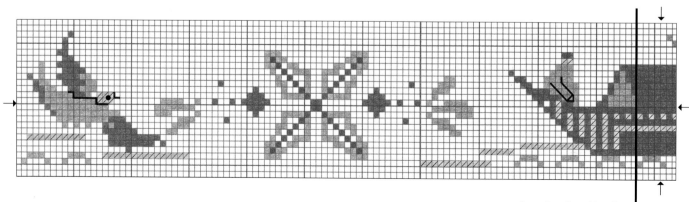

overlap pattern from this point ▷

**for white towel
stranded cottons**

DMC	Anchor	Skeins
797	143	1
799	145	1
336	149	1
341	117	1

French knots

DMC	Anchor
336	149

Backstitch

DMC	Anchor
336	149

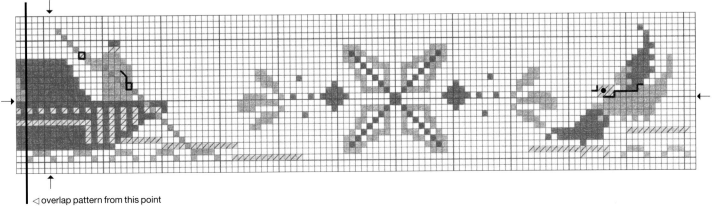

◁ overlap pattern from this point

chapter 3 **the bathroom**

pin. (Most towels have a flat woven strip across their width about 8cm (3⅛in) up from the ends of the towel, and the pin marking the centre of the towel should be placed just next to it.)

With right sides up, place the centre of the band on the centre of the towel over the flat woven strip. Pin, tack and machine topstitch the embroidered Aida onto the towel, leaving the raw edges free at each end. It is best to have the bobbin thread the same colour as the towel and the top thread white to match the Aida.

Turn the raw ends of the Aida to the back of the towel, folding over twice to hide the raw edges. Pin, tack and slipstitch to the towel by hand.

for blue towel

stranded cottons

DMC	Anchor	Skeins
797	143	1
793	176	1
341	117	1

Backstitch

DMC	Anchor
797	143

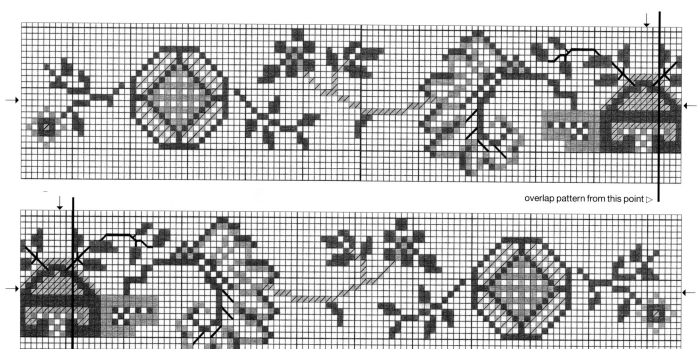

overlap pattern from this point ▷

◁ overlap pattern from this point

chapter 3 **the bathroom**

Dutch Delft bathmat

The inspiration for this unusual bathmat design came from a delicate pair of Dutch Delft shoes. These were given to a friend of mine as a special gift and are on show among her collection of blue and white ceramics. The bathmat features a shoe at each end, facing opposite ways. I feel the shoe motif is particularly appropriate for a bathmat, but see how long it takes your family and friends to make the connection.

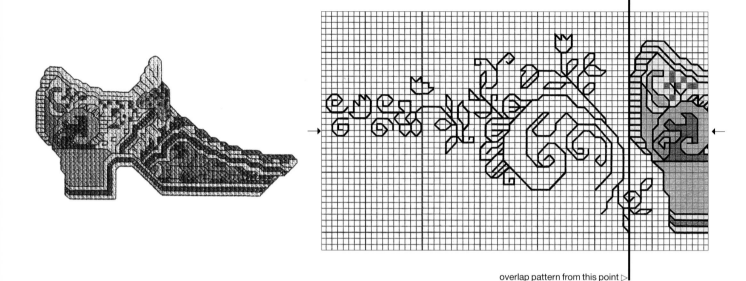

overlap pattern from this point ▷

measurements

Worked on 14 count Aida, the finished embroidery measures 30.2 x 6.3cm (11⅞ x 2½in). Use 2 strands in the needle for cross stitch and for backstitch on the flowers and toe of the shoe. Use one strand in the needle for backstitch outline detail on the shoe and French knots. Work French knots with 2 twists around the needle.

materials

To work the embroidery:
• 2 pieces of 14 count white Aida, 40.5 x 23cm (16 x 9in)
• Stranded cotton embroidery threads as specified in the colour key
• Tapestry needle size 24 or 26

To make up the bathmat:
• Piece of thick white towelling, enough to cut 2 pieces each measuring 71 x 40.5cm (28¼ x 16in)
• White sewing thread
• Basic sewing kit
• Sewing machine

to work the embroidery

Start stitching at the centre of the design and in the centre of each piece of Aida, following the chart. To treat the finished embroideries, see page 103.

to make up the bathmat

Cut out 2 pieces of white towelling, each one measuring 71 x 40.5cm (28¼ x 16in).

Cut the strips of embroidered Aida to 12.5cm (5in) wide, making sure there is 3cm (1⅛in) clear on either side of the widest part of the embroidered shoe to allow for a 1cm (⅜in) seam allowance. Secure the raw edges with zigzag stitch.

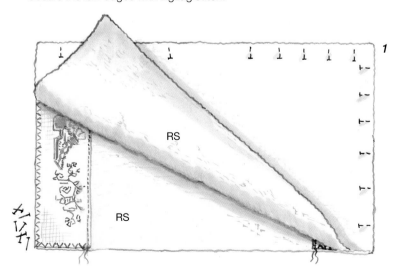

1

◁ overlap pattern from this point

Place one of the towelling pieces on a flat surface, right side up. Lay the 2 prepared pieces of embroidered Aida along the short ends of the towelling, right side up, placing the soles of the shoes towards the ends of the towelling.

Turn in the top raw edges of the embroidered Aida pieces (facing towards the centre of the towelling) by 1cm (⅜in). Pin and tack the turned-in edges to the towelling, at the same time pinning and tacking the other 3 raw edges of the Aida to the raw edges of the towel. Machine topstitch the turned-in edges into place (1). Turn over the towelling and gently press flat.

Lay the second piece of towelling on top of the embroidered piece, right sides together. Pin, tack and machine stitch around the edges with a 1.5cm (⅝in) seam allowance, leaving a gap of about 15cm (6in) halfway down one long side. Trim the excess seam allowance, cutting the corner points at an angle. Pull the mat to the right side through the gap. Pin, tack and slipstitch the gap closed by hand. Press gently, with steam, from the back of the mat.

stranded cottons

	DMC	Anchor	Skeins
■	824	143	2
■	793	176	2
■	792	177	2
■	809	175	2
□	3756	1037	2

French knots

	DMC	Anchor
●	824	143

Backstitch

	DMC	Anchor
▭	809	175 (by toe of shoe)
▬	792	177 (flowers)
▬	824	143 (outline detail on shoe)

Alternatively, you can use a ready-made bathmat. Make sure your Aida strips are at least 4cm (1½in) longer than the width of the mat to allow for neatening and finishing off the ends. Place the embroidered Aida as suggested above and turn in the top and bottom raw edges. Pin, tack and machine topstitch. For turning back and finishing off the raw ends, see the Willow Pattern Hand Towels on page 62.

The bedroom

Be soothed to sleep in a calming bedroom decorated in shades of the healing colour blue. Scatter your bed with appealing Dutch Delft tile cushions and lay your head to rest on a pretty embroidered pillowcase. An accessory bag embellished with a Willow Pattern design and a beautiful

Toile de Jouy-inspired dressing table mat complete the romantic ensemble. Lie back and relax!

There are plenty of options for expanding this blue and white design theme. Using waste canvas, you can stitch the pillowcase design onto the edges of a sheet, duvet cover or bedspread – or even onto a cool white curtain to match the bedlinen. Adapt the dressing table mat design for a smart bolster cushion, or transfer it onto wide ties to wrap around billowing blue or white curtains.

Flowered pillowcase

This delightful design was taken from the same tea plates I used as the source for the Birds Scatter Cushion on page 10. I was inspired by the flowers surrounding the birds on the plates and translated the pattern into this detailed design for a pillowcase.

measurements

Worked on 14 count waste canvas, the finished embroidery measures 10.5 x 10cm (4¼ x 4in). Use 2 strands of cotton in the needle throughout, and work French knots with one twist around the needle.

materials

To work the embroidery:

• White cotton pillowcase
• 2 pieces of 14 count waste canvas, each 14 x 14cm (5½ x 5½in)
• 2 pieces of tear-away medium-weight interfacing, each 14 x 14cm (5½ x 5½in)
• Stranded cotton embroidery threads as specified in the colour key
• Tapestry needle size 24 or 26
• Basic sewing kit

to work the embroidery

Mark the position of the designs by tacking the centre lines of each embroidery straight onto the pillowcase: one in the top right-hand corner and the other in the bottom left-hand corner. Leave enough of a margin to enable you to place your embroidery hoop comfortably around the area to be stitched (1).

Mark in the centre lines on both pieces of waste canvas (2), and place each one on top of one of the embroidery positions marked on the pillowcase. Match the corresponding centre lines and tack the canvas into position (3). Place a piece of tear-away interfacing under each prepared embroidery position and secure by tacking around the edges (see page 100).

Start stitching at the centre of each design and in the centre of each piece of waste canvas, following the charts. When the stitching is complete, remove the waste canvas and tear-away interfacing (see page 100). To treat the finished embroideries, see page 103.

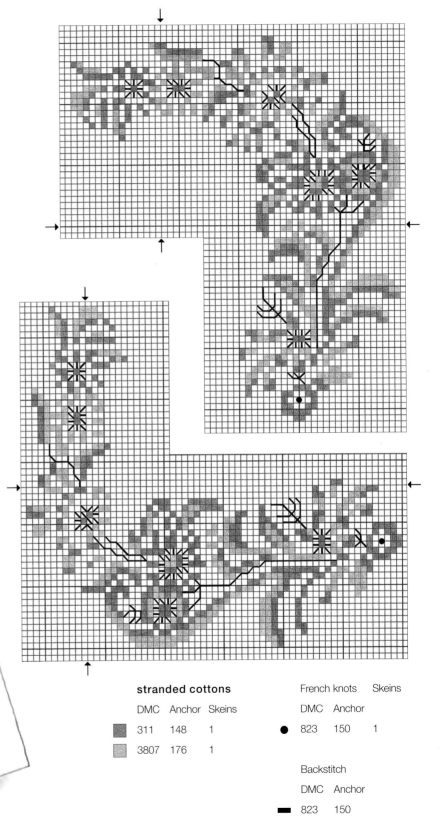

stranded cottons

DMC	Anchor	Skeins
311	148	1
3807	176	1

French knots Skeins

DMC	Anchor	
823	150	1

Backstitch

DMC	Anchor
823	150

Toile de jouy dressing table mat

Bring romance to the bedroom with this pretty dressing table mat, designed in the style of Toile de Jouy. Matching ceramic accessories would complete the picture.

measurements
Worked on 16 count Aida, the finished embroidery measures 15 x 12cm (6 x 4¾in). Use 2 strands in the needle for cross stitch and one strand for backstitch.

materials
To work the embroidery:
• Piece of 16 count white Aida, 40 x 26cm (15¾ x 10¼in)
• Stranded cotton embroidery threads as specified in the colour key
• Tapestry needle size 24 or 26
To make up the mat:
• Piece of white cotton fabric, 40 x 26cm (15¾ x 10¼in)
• White sewing thread
• Basic sewing kit
• Sewing machine

to work the embroidery
Place the design so that the ladies' backs are facing the short sides of the mat. Start stitching at the centre of the design and in the centre of the Aida, following the chart. To treat the finished embroidery, see page 103.

to make up the mat

Cut off 0.3cm (⅛in) from the long sides of the piece of white cotton fabric. This will prevent the lining showing on the right side of the fabric when the mat is complete.

On the embroidered Aida and on the white fabric, mark in 2cm (¾in) from the short ends at each long side. Pin and tack in the seam lines along the long sides with a 1cm (⅜in) seam allowance. Place the Aida and white fabric right sides together and machine stitch together, following the tacked seam lines (1). Trim the excess seam allowances.

Turn the mat to the right side through one of the ends. Press to neaten on the back of the mat.

Machine topstitch down the short ends of the mat with a 2cm (¾in) seam allowance. Cut away the raw edge stitches and fringe both layers of fabric. Trim the fringed ends to neaten. Press.

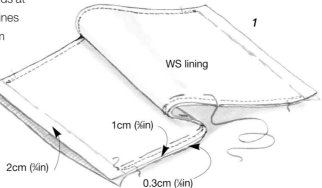

1

WS lining

1cm (⅜in)

2cm (¾in)

0.3cm (⅛in)

stranded cottons

	DMC	Anchor	Skeins
	792	177	1
	793	179	1
	794	175	1
	775	975	1

Backstitch

	DMC	Anchor	
	336	149	1

Willow Pattern accessory bag

This useful bag, inspired by the classic Willow Pattern, is a handy size and just right for storing hair accessories, bangles and beads, or even pretty underwear.

measurements

Worked on 14 count Aida, the finished embroidery measures 26 x 20.5cm (10¼ x 8in). Use 2 strands of cotton in the needle for cross stitch and French knots in the border. Use one strand for backstitch and French knots for the birds' eyes. Work all French knots with 2 twists around the needle.

materials

To work the embroidery:
- Piece of 14 count white Aida, 28 x 33cm (11 x 13in)
- Stranded cotton embroidery threads as specified in the colour key
- Tapestry needle size 24 or 26

To make up the bag:
- Tracing paper for pattern
- 1.5m (1¾yd) white cotton fabric, 114cm (45in) wide
- Piece of interfacing, 18 x 5cm (7 x 2in)
- 1m (39½in) length of navy blue satin ribbon, 1.5cm (⅝in) wide
- Basic sewing kit
- Sewing machine

to work the embroidery

Start stitching at the centre of the design and in the centre of the Aida, following the chart. To treat the finished embroidery, see page 103.

to make up the bag

CUTTING OUT

Following the pattern diagram, make a tracing paper pattern for the bag. Pin the pattern to the white cotton fabric and cut out 2 pieces for the lining, one piece for the front of the bag and one piece for the back. Before unpinning the pattern, mark in all 4 buttonholes and the pocket position on the bag front piece, and the 2 outer button-holes on the bag back piece.

From white cotton fabric, cut out one pocket lining measuring 24 x 30cm (9⅜ x 12in) and a strip for the hanging loop measuring 28 x 4cm (11 x 1½in). These measurements include 1.5cm (⅝in) seam allowances on the short ends.

HANGING LOOP

Join the short ends of the loop piece by machine, right sides together. Press the seam open. Fold the loop in half lengthways, wrong sides together, and press. Tuck in the raw edges to the inside and pin, tack and machine topstitch close to the open edge. This will make a circular tape for the loop.

POCKET

Trim the embroidered Aida to the same size as the pocket lining. Place the pocket lining on the Aida, right sides together, and pin, tack and machine stitch together at the top edge with a 1.5cm (⅝in) seam allowance. Turn to the wrong side and press the seam allowances towards the lining side. Turn to the right side and machine topstitch the seam allowances down onto the lining, about 0.3cm (⅛in) from the seam line.

Fold the lining over onto the embroidered Aida, right sides together. Pin, tack and machine stitch down both sides with a 1.5cm (⅝in) seam allowance, leaving a 2 square width of Aida on

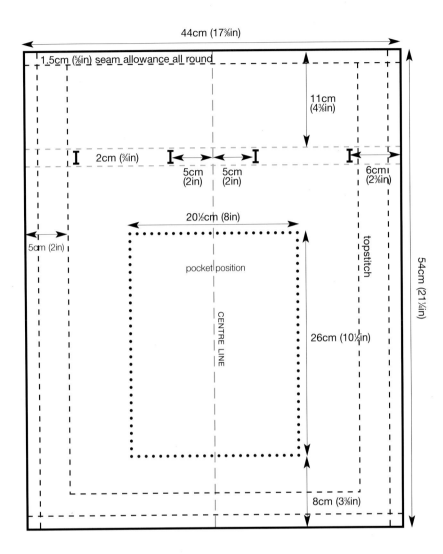

either side of the embroidery. This avoids stitching over the design when topstitching the pocket to the bag. Leave the bottom end open. Trim the sewn seam allowances.

Turn the pocket right side out and press gently with the design facing down on a towel to protect the embroidery.

Turn in the bottom raw edges of the pocket by 1.5cm (⅝in) and press, pin, and tack together. Press once more.

Pin, tack and machine stitch the pocket into position on the front of the bag, stitching as close to the edge of the pocket as possible. Avoid sewing on the embroidery.

chapter 4 **the bedroom**

stranded cottons

DMC	Anchor	Skeins
336	149	2
792	177	2
793	176	1
794	121	1
800	120	1
3756	1037	1
318	253	1

French knots

DMC	Anchor	
336	149	2
939	152	1

Back stitch

DMC	Anchor	
336	149 (border)	
939	152 (birds' eyes	

ASSEMBLY

Lay the back piece of the bag on top of the front piece, right sides together. Pin, tack and machine the side seams. Press and turn right side out.

Pin a small piece of interfacing behind each marked buttonhole, cutting the interfacing slightly larger than the buttonhole. Make the buttonholes, stitching them from the right side of the fabric (see page 105).

Place the 2 bag lining pieces right sides together, then pin, tack and machine stitch the side seams. Press the seam allowances flat, but do not turn the bag lining to the right side.

Slip the lining over the top of the bag, with the wrong side of the lining showing and right sides together. Pin, tack and machine stitch the top edges of the lining and bag together.

Push the lining through to the inside of the bag. Press the top edge and side seams carefully. Tack the bag to the lining around the bottom edge, but still leaving the bottom of the bag open. Turn the bag inside out.

Pin, tack and machine stitch the bottom of the bag, sewing from side seam to side seam. Turn the bag right side out. Press flat, especially around the seam edges. Try to avoid too much pressing on the embroidered pocket.

TUNNELLING

To make the tunnelling, sew 2 lines of stitching above and below the buttonholes as marked on the pattern, 2cm (¾in) apart. On the bag front, sew from the side buttonhole to the centre buttonhole, leave a gap of 10cm (4in), then repeat on the other side of the bag front. Repeat on the back of the bag, but sewing straight across from buttonhole to buttonhole without a gap (1).

FINISHING

Mark the topstitching line shown on the pattern by measuring 3.5cm (1⅜in) in from the outside finished edge of the sides and bottom of the bag, tacking just inside the measurement required. Machine topstitch just outside the tacking line – this makes it easier to pull out the tacking when stitching is complete.

Machine stitch the hanging loop onto the centre back of the bag, just above the tunnelling. Sew 2 lines of machine stitches across the loop, about 2cm (¾in) apart, using the reverse stitch to keep the stitching strong.

Thread the ribbon through the buttonholes (see page 106), starting from one side of the centre front and ending at the other (2). Draw up the ribbon and tie in a bow.

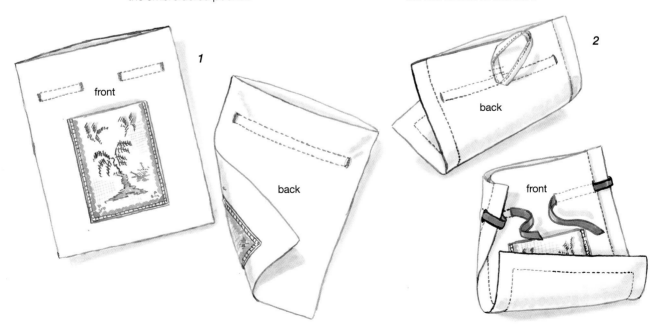

Frilled tile cushion

The lively designs on this and the Piped Tile Cushion on page 81 were taken from two Dutch tiles depicting children playing old-fashioned games. This pretty frilled version would make a charming addition to any girl's bedroom.

measurements
Worked on 14 count Aida, the finished embroidery measures 17 x 17cm (6¾ x 6¾in). Use 2 strands of cotton in the needle for cross stitch and one strand for backstitch.

materials
To work the embroidery:
• Piece of 14 count white Aida, 25.5 x 25.5cm (10 x 10in)
• Stranded cotton embroidery threads as specified in the colour key
• Tapestry needle size 24 or 26
To make up the cushion:
• 1.5m (1¾yd) white cotton fabric, 90cm (36in) wide
• White sewing thread
• 46cm (18in) cushion pad
• Basic sewing kit
• Sewing machine

stranded cottons

DMC	Anchor	Skeins
792	177	1
793	176	1
794	129	1

Backstitch

DMC	Anchor	Skeins
797	133	1

to work the embroidery

Start stitching at the centre of the design and in the centre of the Aida, following the chart. To treat the finished embroidery, see page 103.

chapter 4 **the bedroom**

to make up the cushion

Cut 2 pieces of white cotton fabric, each one measuring 46 x 46cm (18 x 18in).

Cut strips of the same fabric, 12cm (4¾in) wide, to make a strip 3.68m (4yd) long when joined. This will fit twice around the square of the cushion to make the outer frill.

Cut sufficient strips of fabric, 12cm (4¾in) wide, to make a strip 140cm (56in) long when joined. This will fit twice around the square of the trimmed embroidery to make the inner frill.

Tack in the centre lines on the cushion front piece. Trim the excess Aida fabric around the embroidery to leave one to two squares free and a 1.5cm (⅝in) seam allowance, and secure the raw edges with zigzag stitch. Tack in the centre lines on the Aida and turn back the edges, tacking them down to the back of the embroidery.

Join the outer frill strips for the cushion to make a long strip. Repeat for the frill around the embroidery. Fold each of the frill strips in half lengthways and sew 2 lines of stitching along the raw edge to make gathers (see page 107).

Pin the raw edges of the shorter gathered frill to the back of the embroidery and tack into position (1). Pin, tack and machine stitch the 2 ends to join them together. Trim and zigzag stitch or overcast the raw edges to secure, making sure they are not visible on the right side.

Pin, tack and machine topstitch the embroidered piece to the centre of the front cushion piece. Lay the remaining frill on the right side of the cushion front, raw edge to raw edge and the folded edge of the frill towards the centre. Pin, tack and machine topstitch down, joining the frill ends in the same manner as for the first frill.

Sandwich the frill between the front and the back cushion pieces, placing right sides together. Pin, tack and machine stitch with a 1cm (⅜in) seam allowance, rounding off the corners and leaving a gap of about 25.5cm (10in) at the top of the cushion (2). Trim the excess seam allowances and pull the cushion cover through the gap to the right side. Insert the cushion pad and slipstitch the gap closed.

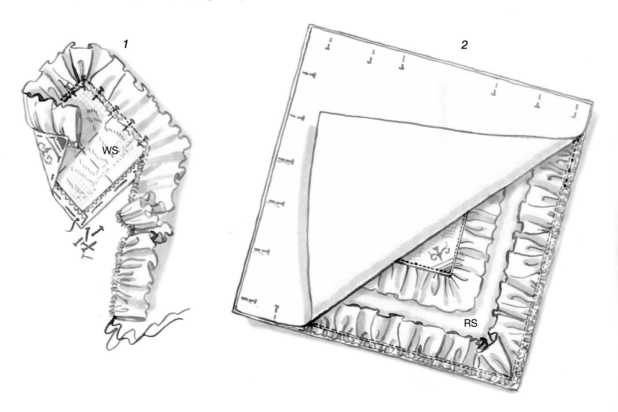

Piped tile cushion

Similar in design to the Frilled Tile Cushion on page 78 and with the embroidery motif taken from a matching Dutch tile showing two small boys bowling hoops, this small square cushion would add a touch of style to a young boy's bedroom. Both the cross-stitch motif and the edge of the cushion itself are outlined by a border of piping and finished with a neat knot. The skipping design on page 78 and this hooping bowling motif could also be used in combination to decorate a pair of matching cushions.

measurements

Worked on 14 count Aida, the finished embroidery measures 17.5 x 17.5cm (6⅞ x 6⅞in). Use 2 strands of cotton in the needle for cross stitch and one strand for backstitch.

materials

To work the embroidery:
- Piece of 14 count pale blue Aida, 25.5 x 25.5cm (10 x 10in)
- Stranded cotton embroidery threads as specified in the colour key
- Tapestry needle size 24 or 26

To make up the cushion:
- 1m (1¼yd) blue cotton or linen fabric, 90cm (36in) wide
- 2 lengths of blue cord, 112cm (44in) for embroidered square and 225cm (108in) for cushion edge
- Adhesive tape
- Stranded cotton embroidery thread to match cord
- Blue sewing thread
- 46cm (18in) cushion pad
- Basic sewing kit
- Sewing machine

to work the embroidery

Start stitching at the centre of the design and in the centre of the Aida, following the chart. To treat the finished embroidery, see page 103.

to make up the cushion

Cut 2 pieces of blue fabric, each measuring 46 x 46cm (18 x 18in).

Cut 4 strips of the same fabric, each measuring 82.5 x 5cm (32½ x 2in).

Cut another 4 strips of the same fabric, each measuring 34.5 x 5cm (13½ x 2in).

Sew up each strip separately by joining the short ends, right sides together, to make 8 separate rings. Press the seams flat and turn each ring to the right side, placing the seam in the centre of the strip. Press the ring flat. Fold in half, long edges together, and tack the raw edges together. This makes the tubes to take the piping.

Prepare the embroidered Aida in the same way as for the Frilled Tile Cushion (see page 78). Instead of tacking a frill behind the Aida, tack the 4 shorter tubes behind the edges, about 0.5cm (¼in) in from each corner. Tack in the centre lines on the front cushion piece. Pin, tack and machine topstitch the prepared square to the centre of the

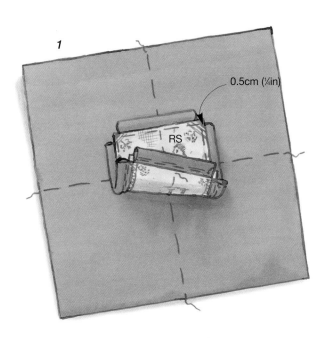

1

0.5cm (¼in)

RS

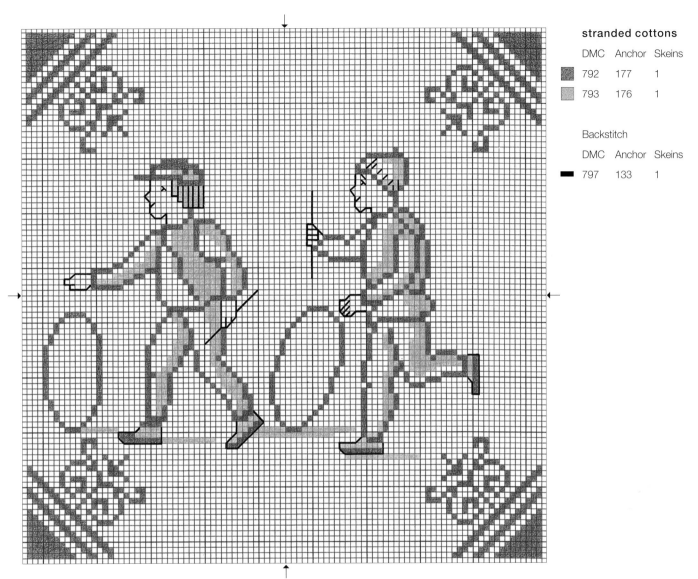

stranded cottons

DMC	Anchor	Skeins
■ 792	177	1
▨ 793	176	1

Backstitch

DMC	Anchor	Skeins
▬ 797	133	1

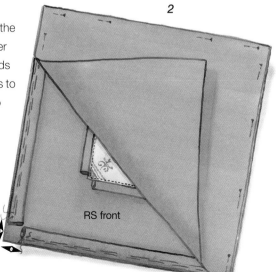

2

RS front

2cm (¾in)

front cushion piece (1).

Pin and tack the larger tubes to the edge of the front cushion piece, raw edges to raw edges and with the folds facing in towards the centre of the cushion, about 2cm (¾in) from each corner (2). Sandwich the tubes between the front and the back cushion pieces, placing right sides together and join the front and back in the same way as for the Frilled Tile Cushion (see page 78). Insert the cushion pad and slipstitch the gap closed by hand.

Wrap a small piece of adhesive tape around the ends of each of the cords to prevent fraying. Thread the shorter cord through the centre tubes (see page 106) and knot the ends. Repeat for the outer tubes. Knot the loose ends and cut both sets of ends to an appropriate length. To finish, wind a length of embroidery thread the same colour as the cord around each cord a short distance from the end, securing with a few stitches.

Accessories and gifts

You can use your embroidery skills to make extra special gifts for the many important people in your life. These will be kept and treasured long after mass-produced items have been forgotten, some even becoming family heirlooms that are handed down through generations.

The bell pull, for example, would make an ideal present for a member of the family whose hobby is sailing. Or, if your relatives tend to choose less active pastimes, the

windmill picture would be perfect for a Delft pottery enthusiast, complementing the ceramics in their collection.

The Willow Pattern sampler offers a variety of motifs that could be borrowed to make gift cards, trinket box tops or perhaps a set of coasters for a keen collector of the willow design. Use the Asiatic pheasant scented sachet embroidery to make a delightful sleep cushion for an elderly relative. Finally, if you find the photo frame too daunting a project, the designs would translate very easily onto table or bedlinen using waste canvas, to make a truly memorable gift.

Windmill picture

This design came from the same liquor jar as the Dutch Delft Pot Holder on page 43, the main design on the jar being a windmill. The mark on the bottom of the jar is 'HJ75a', so it probably came from the Herman Jansen distillers, who have been in business at Schiedham in Holland since 1717.

measurements

Worked on 14 count Aida, the finished embroidery measures 18 x 22cm (7 x 8⅝in). Use 2 strands of cotton in the needle throughout.

materials

To work the embroidery:
• Piece of 14 count white Aida, 30.5 x 30.5cm
   (12 x 12in)
• Stranded cotton embroidery threads as
   specified in the colour key
• Tapestry needle size 24 or 26
To make up the picture:
• Picture frame
• Masking tape
• Acid-free mounting board
• Strong thread and large needle

▷

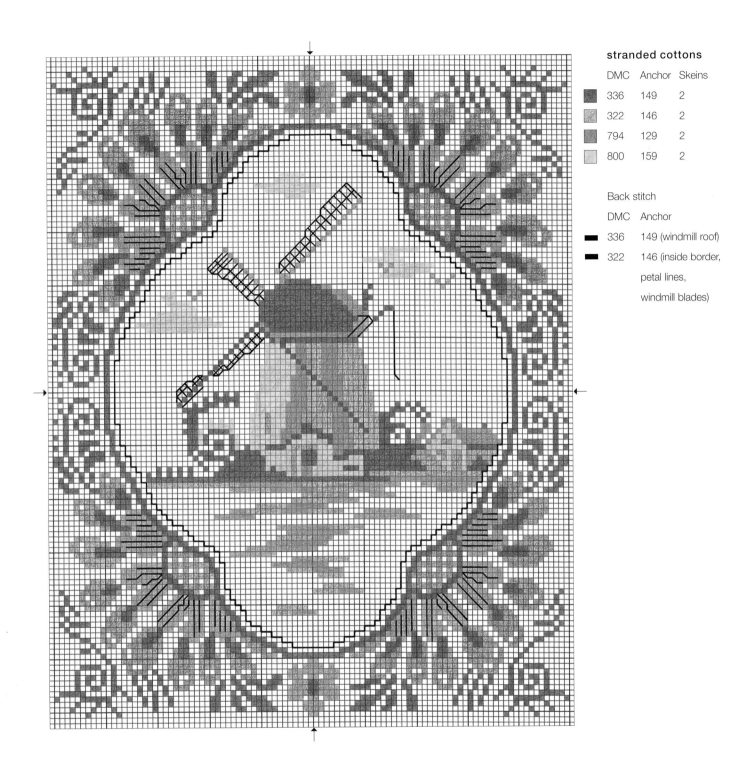

stranded cottons

	DMC	Anchor	Skeins
■	336	149	2
▨	322	146	2
▨	794	129	2
▨	800	159	2

Back stitch

	DMC	Anchor	
▬	336	149	(windmill roof)
▬	322	146	(inside border,
			petal lines,
			windmill blades)

to work the embroidery

Start stitching at the centre of the design and in the centre of the Aida, following the chart. To treat the finished embroidery, see page 103.

to frame the picture

Frame the picture following the instructions given on page 107. Alternatively, you can take it to a professional framer.

Willow Pattern sampler

I have used two different variations on
the classic willow design as sources for this
sampler. One design came from my old soup
bowl, marked 'Old Willow', the other from
a friend's plate marked 'Real Old Willow'!

measurements
Worked on 14 count Aida, the finished embroidery
measures 17 x 21cm (6¾ x 8¼in). Use 2 strands of
cotton in the needle throughout, and work French
knots with 2 twists around the needle.

materials
To work the embroidery:
• Piece of 14 count antique white Aida,
  32 x 28cm (12½ x 11in)
• Stranded cotton embroidery threads as
  specified in the colour key
• Tapestry needle size 24 or 26
To make up the sampler:
• Picture frame
• Acid-free mounting board
• Masking tape
• Strong thread and large needle

to work the embroidery
Start stitching at the centre of the design and in the
centre of the Aida, following the chart. To treat the
finished embroidery, see page 103. ▷

stranded cottons			stranded cottons			French knots		Backstitch	
DMC	Anchor	Skeins	DMC	Anchor	Skeins	DMC	Anchor	DMC	Anchor
796	134	2	809	175	2	796	134	796	134 (main areas)
3807	176	2	3752	1032	2			3807	176 (bridge)

chapter 5 **accessories and gifts**

to frame the sampler

Frame the sampler following the instructions given on page 107. Alternatively, you can take it to a professional framer.

for alphabet

stranded cottons

	DMC	Anchor	Skeins
■	796	134	1

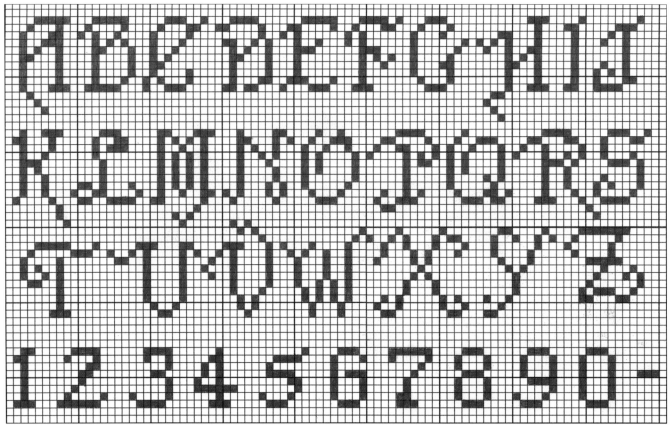

Willow Pattern photo frame

The design for this photo frame came from a Wedgwood plate of mine that is decorated in Willow Pattern style, but without the birds. I used the highly decorated floral rim as inspiration for the photo frame, translating the design into a shape that fitted the chunky rectangle of the frame.

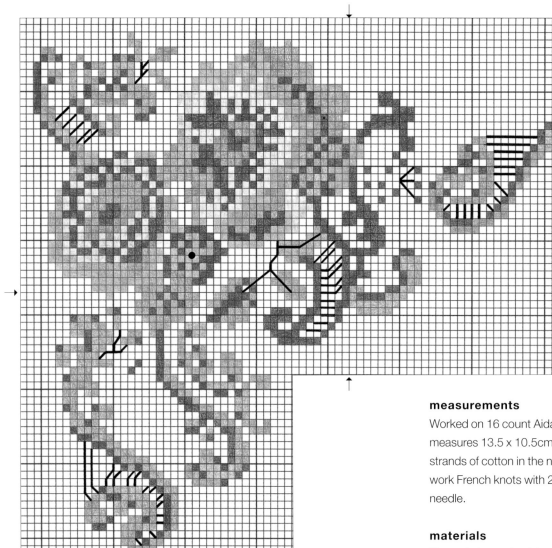

stranded cottons

DMC	Anchor	Skeins
796	134	2
793	176	2
341	117	2
3747	120	2

French knots

DMC	Anchor
● 796	134

Backstitch

DMC	Anchor
▬ 796	134

measurements

Worked on 16 count Aida, the finished embroidery measures 13.5 x 10.5cm (5¾ x 4¼in). Use 2 strands of cotton in the needle throughout, and work French knots with 2 twists around the needle.

materials

To work the embroidery:
• Piece of 16 count antique white Aida, 36 x 50cm (14 x 19½in)
• Tracing paper for template
• Stranded cotton embroidery threads as specified in the colour key
• Tapestry needle size 24 or 26

To make up the frame:
• Photo frame 27.2 x 22.5cm (10½ x 8⅞in), 7cm (2¾in) wide
• Double-sided adhesive tape, 5cm (2in) wide
• Piece of thick wadding, same measurements as photo frame
• Iron-on interfacing, 19 x 14.2cm (7½ x 5⅝in)
• Superglue
• A3 cream paper or felt, same measurements as photo frame
• 89cm (35in) length of coloured cord (optional)
• Basic sewing kit

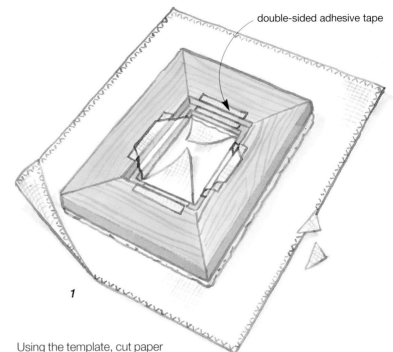

double-sided adhesive tape

1

to work the embroidery

If you cannot find a frame exactly the correct size,
ask a picture framer to make one up for you.

Trace off the photo frame template on page
109. Tack in the horizontal and vertical centre lines
on the Aida fabric. Pin the template to the Aida,
matching the centre lines, and tack in the frame
shape through the template.

In the top left-hand corner of the frame shape,
tack in the centre lines for the embroidery position.
Turn the fabric around and repeat the process for
the bottom right-hand corner. For each of the
placements, start stitching at the centre of the
design and at the centre point marked on the Aida,
following the chart. To treat the finished embroidery,
see page 103.

to make up the frame

Stick pieces of double-sided adhesive tape onto
the right side of the frame and place the thick
wadding on top.

Iron the interfacing to the back and centre of the
embroidered Aida, in the area where the photo will
be placed, to prevent the fabric fraying when the
centre is cut. Pin the Aida right side up onto the
wadding.

Turn the whole frame over and cut diagonal
lines in the Aida, from each corner but not quite
reaching to the point, through the centre of the
area that will be the space for the photograph.

Stick double-sided adhesive tape to the ledge
where the glass will be placed and on the back of
the frame. Gently pull back the diagonally cut
pieces of Aida, manoeuvring them into position and
sticking them onto the adhesive tape (1).

Stick more double-side adhesive tape around
the outside back of the frame. Pull the outside
edges of the Aida to the back of the frame,
manoeuvring them into position. Fold down the
excess fabric in the corners, pinning to keep it in
position (2). Superglue down under the folds,
taking care to avoid the pins, otherwise they will
be stuck fast.

Using the template, cut paper
or felt to shape to cover the back of the
frame, leaving just the photo-fitting space free.
Stick more double-sided adhesive tape over the
back of the frame and stick the paper or hand sew
the felt onto the back of the frame to neaten.

If using, place the cream cord around the front
inner edge of the frame, supergluing it as you go.
Leave enough cord free at both ends and enough
space in one corner to tie the
cord in a bow.

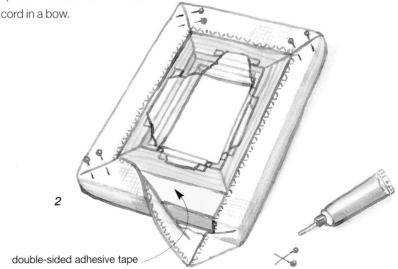

2

double-sided adhesive tape

English Delft bell pull

As a gift for someone interested in sailing, embroider this tranquil scene – inspired by an English Delft tile – onto a bell pull. I found a real goat's bell in a market to complete the pull, but you can use any design of bell to add the finishing touch.

measurements

Worked on 14 count Aida, the finished embroidery measures 11 x 28.5cm (4⅜ x 11¼in) for the bell pull and 5.5 x 2cm (2¼ x ¾in) for the loop. Use 2 strands of cotton in the needle for cross stitch and one strand for backstitch. Use one strand for French knots with 2 twists around the needle.

materials
To work the embroidery:
• 2 pieces of 14 count antique white Aida, 38 x 18cm (15 x 7in) for bell pull and 14 x 14cm (5½ x 5½in) for bell loop
• Stranded cotton embroidery threads as specified in the colour key
• Tapestry needle size 24 or 26

To make up the bell pull:

- 20cm (8in) wooden bell pull end
- Navy blue acrylic paint
- 1.3cm (½in) bristle paintbrush
- Tracing paper for template
- Piece of cream calico fabric, 43 x 25.5cm (17 x 10in)
- Piece of stiff interfacing, 43 x 25.5cm (17 x 10in)
- 80cm (31½in) length of narrow cream cord
- Bell of your choice
- 2 wooden beads with holes large enough to take narrow cord
- Cream sewing thread
- Basic sewing kit
- Sewing machine

to work the embroidery

For each piece, start stitching at the centre of the design and in the centre of the Aida, following the colour chart. To treat the finished embroideries, see page 103.

stranded cottons

	DMC	Anchor	Skeins
■	3750	150	1
◩	824	142	1
▨	825	142	1
▨	334	145	1
◿	809	175	1
▨	827	159	1

French knots

	DMC	Anchor
●	3750	150

Backstitch

	DMC	Anchor
▬	3750	150

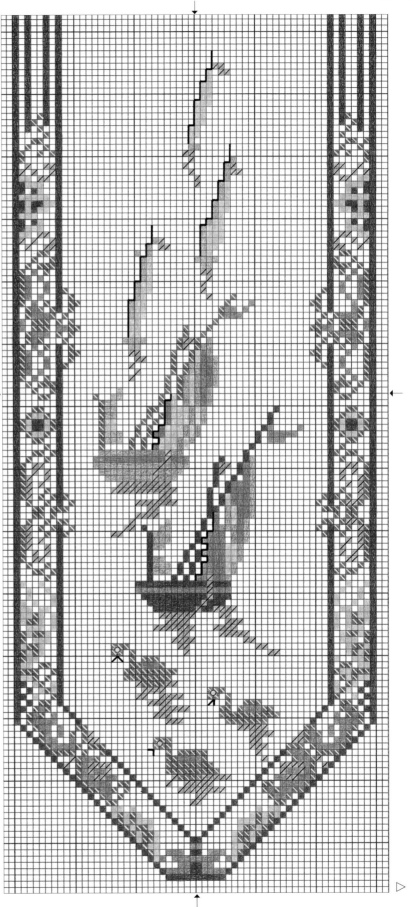

to make up the bell pull

Remove one of the wooden knobs from the wooden bell pull end and cut the rod to 14.2cm (5⅝in). Paint the wooden bell pull end and the 2 wooden beads with navy blue acrylic paint and leave to dry.

Trace off the bell pull and bell loop templates on pages 108–109. Tack in the long centre line on both pieces of embroidered Aida. Pin the templates onto their corresponding embroideries, matching up the centre lines, and cut the Aida to shape.

Using the bell pull template, cut out one piece in calico and one piece in stiff interfacing. Secure the raw edges of the calico and both pieces of Aida with zigzag stitch. Pin the interfacing to the wrong side of the calico. Using large machine stitches, join the layers together around the raw edges with a 1.5cm (⅝in) seam allowance.

Turn one long edge of the embroidered bell loop, right side out, to the back. Turn the other long edge to the back, folding in the raw edge by 1cm (⅜in). Pin and tack on top of the other raw edge and slipstitch together by hand.

With right sides together and the loop pointing towards the other end of the bell pull, pin, tack and machine topstitch the loop onto the point of the bell pull, matching up the design of the two pieces as closely as possible.

Pin, tack and machine stitch the calico onto the embroidery, with right sides together and the interfacing facing up. Using a 1cm (⅜in) seam allowance, start stitching from the top of one long side, around the point, and back up to the top of the opposite seam, sewing on the wrong side of the Aida and about 3 squares outside the edge of the embroidery. Leave the top end open. Keep the loop inside the sewing (1).

Trim the excess seam allowances and pull through to the right side. Press to neaten. Zigzag stitch the top open layers together and turn about 2.5cm (1in) of fabric over the wooden bell pull rod

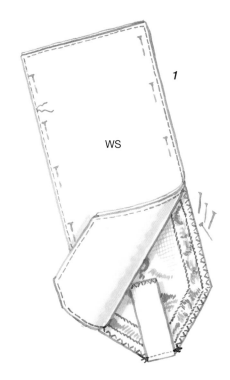

towards the back, to make a tunnel. Pin and mark the position of the tunnel. Pull out the wooden rod and machine topstitch the tunnel down. Push the rod through the tunnel and replace the knob.

Slot the loop through the loop of the bell, passing it through to the back of the bell pull. Slipstitch the loop into position by hand.

Double the cord and tie it around the wooden bell pull end. Leave the ends loose and place a blue-painted wooden bead on each end. Knot neatly to secure (2).

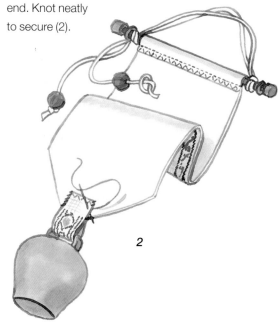

Asiatic pheasant scented sachet

The Asiatic pheasant pottery pattern is almost as popular a design as the Willow Pattern. It is paler in colour and was produced by the Brownhill Pottery Co. of Tunstall in Staffordshire, England – a county renowned for its ceramics – from 1872 to 1896. The source for this design was a friend's large platter, from which I chose the central pheasant motif to decorate a charming scented sachet.

measurements

Worked on 16 count Aida, the finished embroidery measures 14 x 14cm (5½ x 5½in). Use 2 strands of cotton in the needle throughout, and work French knots with 2 twists around the needle.

materials

To work the embroidery:
- Piece of 16 count antique white Aida, 23 x 23cm (9 x 9in)
- Stranded cotton embroidery threads as specified in the colour key
- Tapestry needle size 24 or 26

To make up the sachet:
- Piece of cream fine cotton fabric, 114 x 20cm (45 x 8in)
- 120cm (48in) length of cream cord
- Piece of white or cream muslin, 32 x 18cm (12½ x 7in)
- Pot pourri
- Cream sewing thread
- Basic sewing kit
- Sewing machine

stranded cottons

DMC	Anchor	Skeins
824	143	1
793	176	1
341	117	1
3747	120	1

French knots

DMC	Anchor
824	143

Backstitch

DMC	Anchor
824	143

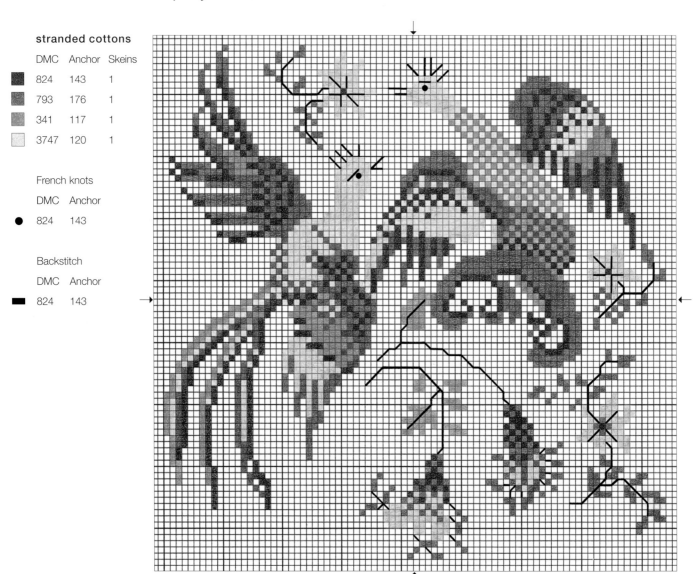

to work the embroidery

Start stitching at the centre of the design and in the centre of the Aida, following the chart. To treat the finished embroidery, see page 103.

to make up the sachet

On the embroidered Aida, mark a line 1cm (⅜in) out from the edge of the embroidery for the finished edge and another line a further 1cm (⅜in) out for the seam allowance. Trim the fabric to the seam allowance mark and secure the raw edges with zigzag stitch. Tuck the seam allowance to the wrong side of the embroidery and tack on all sides.

Take the piece of cream fine cotton fabric and, with right sides together, fold it in half widthways and pin, tack and machine stitch together. Place the stitched seam in the centre and pin, tack and machine down the long side seams, leaving a small gap. Turn this through to the right side through the gap. Press to neaten.

Fold the sewn fabric in half widthways and tack in the centre line on the right side. Place the embroidered Aida on the front of the cotton and pin, tack and machine topstitch it down, 0.5cm from the marked centre line (1). Fold in half, right sides together to resemble a bag. Pin, tack and machine stitch the side seams: sew 9.5cm (3¾in) down from the top, leave a 2cm (¾in) gap, then carry on sewing to the bottom of the bag. Repeat on the opposite seam. Turn the bag right side out.

Fold down the top of the bag to the inside, covering the gaps. Sew tunnelling by machine topstitching around the bag on either side of the 2cm (¾in) gap (2).

Cut the cord into 2 equal lengths and thread these through opposite holes (see page 106). Knot each double end of cord to secure (3).

Fold the piece of muslin in half widthways and pin, tack and machine stitch the side seams. Turn through to the right side and fill with pot pourri. Slipstitch the opening closed by hand or use machine topstitching.

Materials and techniques

This chapter provides all the information you need to work the embroideries in this book and make them up into attractive and useful items for your home. The techniques are all very straightforward, and by following the instructions carefully you will be able to achieve results to be proud of every time.

MATERIALS AND EQUIPMENT
fabrics for cross stitch

The majority of the projects in this book are stitched on a blockweave fabric called Aida, while some of the items use waste canvas.

AIDA

To make a perfect square with each cross stitch, you need to use an evenweave fabric. This means that over a given length the fabric has the same number of threads woven into it vertically (warp) as horizontally (weft), so the cross stitches – and therefore the designs – will not be distorted.

Aida is the easiest fabric on which to work cross stitch embroidery. The weave forms distinct blocks (hence 'blockweave') with relatively large holes in between, making it easy to count and to stitch.

Aida fabric is available in various colours and 'counts'. The count denotes the number of blocks of threads per 2.5cm (1in): Aida ranges from 8 to 18 count. The higher the count, the larger the number of stitches per 2.5cm (1in) and the smaller an embroidery with a given number of stitches will be.

WASTE CANVAS

Using waste canvas allows you to embroider directly onto most fabrics, even if the weave is not even or it is not possible to count the threads. Aida waste canvas is used for the projects in this book and ranges from 8 to 14 count. Tacking this gridded canvas on top of the fabric makes it possible to work the design easily, and the use of tear-away interfacing underneath the fabric stabilizes the embroidery.

To use waste canvas, position the canvas on top of the fabric that you wish to embroider and place the tear-away interfacing underneath, to make a sandwich. Tack securely, then embroider the design through all three layers. When you have finished, trim the waste canvas carefully around the finished embroidery, leaving a margin of 0.5–1cm (¼–⅜in), then moisten the canvas and carefully pull out the canvas threads using tweezers. Remove all the horizontal threads first, followed by all the vertical threads (or vice versa), leaving the cross stitch design in place. Finally, cut or tear away the interfacing.

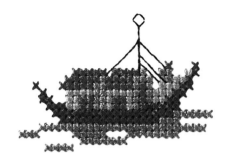

embroidery needles

Tapestry needles have large eyes for ease of threading and blunt points that will not separate and split the fabric threads. A size 24 or 26 needle is suitable for all the projects in this book.

embroidery threads

Several different types of thread are suitable for working cross stitch. However, all the projects in this book were stitched using stranded embroidery cottons. These fine cottons are supplied in a small skein and consist of six strands of thread, loosely twisted together. This enables you to cut off the length of thread you require (no more than about 45cm (18in), otherwise it may tangle while you are stitching), and to use varying numbers of strands in the needle – separate the individual strands and recombine the number required to ensure a good finish to the stitching. The number of strands required is specified for each project; as a general guide, for cross stitch on 14 to 16 count Aida you should use two strands, while on 18 to 20 count you should use one. You can vary the texture of your embroidery by experimenting with different numbers.

STITCHING THE DESIGN
preparing the fabric

Cut the fabric to the size required and secure the raw edges by oversewing with zigzag stitch on your sewing machine or by binding with masking tape.

For each project, the position of the embroidery will vary according the design of the object, but in every case the method for centring the cross stitch design on the Aida fabric is the same. Always leave plenty of spare fabric around the embroidery, particularly with small items that might not otherwise fit an embroidery hoop (see page 102).

CENTRING ON AIDA

To centre the design on Aida, fold the fabric in half both ways, making visible crease lines; the point at which these lines intersect marks the centre of the design. Tack in the two crease lines in a contrasting thread. Match the centre of the chart (see Reading the charts, page 102) to the centre of the marked fabric and start stitching at this point. If the design is not to be placed centrally, then work out the approximate area in which it will be placed from the project instructions, then mark and tack in the vertical and horizontal centre lines of this area.

CENTRING ON WASTE CANVAS

Tack in the centre lines on the fabric you are using, in the same way as on Aida. Since you cannot fold the stiff waste canvas, refer to the project instructions for the dimensions of the finished design and use these as a guide. Your stitching area on the canvas must be greater than these dimensions, and you must allow a margin for fixing the hoop (see page 102). Establish a boundary for the design then mark in the centre lines with a fabric marker or tacking stitches in a contrasting thread. As before, they will cross at the centre point of the canvas. Repeat to mark the centre point of the interfacing. Use the tacking lines to line up all three centre points (on waste canvas, fabric and interfacing). Secure all three layers in a 'sandwich' (see page 100) with firm tacking before starting to stitch.

EMBROIDERY HOOPS

Although it is possible to work your design while holding the fabric in your hand, it is far more satisfactory to use a hoop to keep the work taut and the stitches neat. An embroidery hoop consists of two rings, one smaller than the other. To fix the fabric into the hoop, stretch it over the smaller ring and then place the larger ring over the top, tightening the integral screw to keep the fabric in position. To protect the fabric from being marked by the hard edge of the smaller ring over which it is stretched, it is best to bind the ring with strips of fabric first. Hoops are available in a range of sizes from 10cm (4in) to 30cm (12in) in diameter.

reading the charts

Each project in this book is accompanied by a chart on which each coloured square represents one cross stitch. Backstitch is denoted by a line in black and, in some projects, an additional colour. French knots are shown as a filled black circle. Where there are blank squares in the design, the fabric should be left unstitched.

Where squares are shown divided diagonally, with half the square in one colour and half in another (or left blank), three-quarter and quarter cross stitches are needed. When a divided square is on the edge of the design, work a three-quarter cross stitch to fill in the coloured area shown on the chart. When a square within the design is divided, stitch one part as a three-quarter cross stitch and the other part as a quarter cross stitch.

stranded cottons

DMC	Anchor	Skeins
334	977	1
824	132	1

French knots

DMC	Anchor
336	149

Backstitch

DMC	Anchor	Skeins
336	149	1

Sample chart and colour key

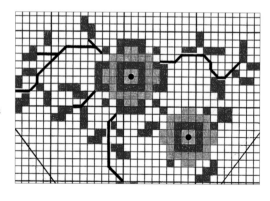

The colours of the chart squares correspond to those in the accompanying colour key, with the numbers alongside indicating the colour codes for the appropriate threads in both DMC and Anchor systems. The designs in this book were stitched with DMC stranded embroidery cottons. The nearest equivalent Anchor thread number has been provided, but if you use Anchor threads your finished work may not match the photographed embroideries exactly.

Before starting to stitch, refer to the chart for the project and check the dimensions of the design given alongside. Find the centre point of the design with the aid of the arrows marked on two sides of the chart. From the vertical arrow, trace a straight line downwards through the chart to the bottom; from the horizontal arrow, trace another straight line across the chart to the other side. Where these lines intersect is the centre of the design.

Start stitching at the centre of the design and keep a careful count of the stitches as you work, following the design accurately. It is best to work each small area of one colour and then change the thread to the next colour to work the adjacent stitches. In this way, you are likely to make fewer mistakes in counting than if you work all the stitches of one colour before changing thread. You may like to use a ruler or a piece of card to mark off each area of the chart as you complete it; this will help you to concentrate on one area at a time.

stitch techniques
CROSS STITCH

To start working in cross stitch, do not tie the thread in a knot, since this will show as an unsightly bump on the finished embroidery and may eventually come undone and loosen the stitches in the design. Instead, secure the thread by sewing one or two backstitches (see below) in an area that will eventually be covered up with cross stitches. Alternatively, leave a tail of thread, holding it in position at the back of the fabric so that it will be caught in the cross stitches as you sew.

Cross stitch

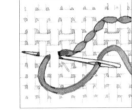
Back stitch

French knots

Quarter cross stitch

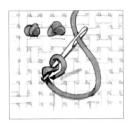
Three-quarter cross stitch

If you are working in a small area and diagonally, it is better to complete each cross stitch before moving on to the next. To work a single cross stitch, bring the needle up through to the front of the fabric at the bottom left of the stitch and take it back down through at the top right. Bring it up again at the top left and take it back down at the bottom right.

If you are working in a large area and horizontally or vertically, work from right to left and from top right to bottom left to make a row of diagonal stitches. When you have worked the correct number of stitches, work back along the row, crossing the diagonal stitches from top left to bottom right.

Whichever way you work, the top stitches of all the crosses must lie in the same direction, otherwise the work will appear uneven.

To secure a new thread and to finish stitching, slide the needle under several stitches already worked and cut off the thread neatly.

BACKSTITCH

This stitch is used to outline and highlight parts of a cross stitch design. Starting with the needle at the back of the fabric, bring the needle up through to the right side of the fabric and make a backward stitch, passing the needle to the back of the fabric. Bring the needle up through to the right side of the fabric again, the length of one stitch ahead of the previous stitch. Continue in this way, following the chart for the direction of the stitches, remembering that the understitch is always twice as long as the top stitch.

FRENCH KNOTS

These are round, raised bobbles that are useful for representing eyes, the centres of flowers and so on. Bring the needle up through to the right side of the fabric in the position of the French knot. Twist the thread around the needle once, twice or three times, depending on the size of knot required. Holding the thread firmly with your thumb, push the needle down through the fabric in a position very close to where it first emerged. Hold down the knot with your thumb. Pull the thread to the wrong side of the fabric and secure the knot with one or two small stitches.

THREE-QUARTER AND QUARTER CROSS STITCH

To work a quarter cross stitch, bring the needle up through to the front of the Aida at the top left and take it back down again in the centre of the Aida square. To work a three-quarter cross stitch, bring the needle up through to the front of the fabric at the top right and back down again at the bottom left, over the quarter cross stitch.

washing and pressing

When you have completed the design and removed all the waste canvas and interfacing, if used, wash the finished embroidery in warm water with a gentle soap powder to remove any dirt that has got onto it during the stitching. To remove moisture, roll the embroidery up in a towel then place it face down on a towel and press on the wrong side of the fabric with an iron on a low setting to flatten the finished embroidery. Allow the work to dry thoroughly before mounting it as a picture or making it up into the finished item.

MAKING UP
basic sewing kit

To make up the projects in this book, you will need the following basic sewing kit. For most, a sewing machine is also required.

- paper scissors
- fabric scissors
- embroidery scissors
- tape measure
- tacking threads
- sewing needles
- tailor's chalk
- pins
- unpicker
- thimble
- safety pins
- tweezers
- fabric marker
- embroidery hoops

measuring and cuting out

PATTERNS AND TEMPLATES

A few of the projects in this book are accompanied by a template or pattern diagram.

The templates are reproduced on pages 108–109. Trace the template onto tracing paper for your chosen project. Mark all seam allowances, notches and balance marks (see below), embroidery positions and so on shown on the template onto the tracing paper version. Pin this tracing paper template to your fabric and cut out around it. Mark the embroidery positions and any other relevant points onto the fabric using tailor's chalk, and snip all notches and balance marks before unpinning the template.

Pattern diagrams are reproduced alongside the instructions for the relevant project. Use the measurements shown on the diagram to make a pattern in tracing paper, marking in all seam allowances, notches and balance marks, and the positions of the embroidery, buttonholes and so on. Pin this tracing paper pattern to your fabric and cut out around it. Mark the embroidery and button-hole positions, and any other relevant points, onto the fabric using tailor's chalk, and snip all notches and balance marks before unpinning the pattern.

Notches are V-shaped marks cut at right angles into the edges of paper patterns and templates, indicating seam allowances. Balance marks are cut in the same way, to ensure accurate joining of fabric pieces. Snip through the notches on paper patterns and templates, cutting into the fabric to transfer the relevant points from the pattern to the fabric. Do not cut into the fabric by more than 0.3cm (⅛in).

seams

For the neatest results, pin and tack all seams before machine stitching. Make the tacking line slightly further out towards the raw edges of the fabric than the seam line, so that the machine stitching does not have to be worked directly on top of it. Once the machine stitching is complete, remove the tacking threads.

When sewing up seams, use the reverse stitch button on your machine to secure the beginning and end of each line of stitching. Start to stitch about 1cm (⅜in) down the seam line. Reverse up to the end before stitching forwards down the seam line to the other end, then reverse back up the stitching line for 1cm (⅜in) to prevent the stitches unravelling later.

Pressing seams flat between each stage of machine stitching will make your work look much crisper. Trim the excess seam allowances to within 0.5cm (¼in) of the stitch line. Relieve bulk at corners by trimming across them at an angle – this will give a sharp point when it is turned to the right side.

Clip into curved seam allowances to prevent the fabric puckering and to allow it to be pressed flat when ironed. Seam allowances that lie on the inside of a curved seam should be notched to get rid of excess fabric and allow the seam to lie smoothly. Cut little V shapes into the seam allowance at intervals, almost to the stitch line. Seam allowances on the outside of a curved seam should be clipped. Cut into the seam allowance at intervals, at right angles and almost to the stitch line. This allows the curve of the seam allowance to spread out and releases the tension in the fabric.

Secure all raw edges on seam allowances with zigzag stitch on your sewing machine, to prevent the fabric fraying.

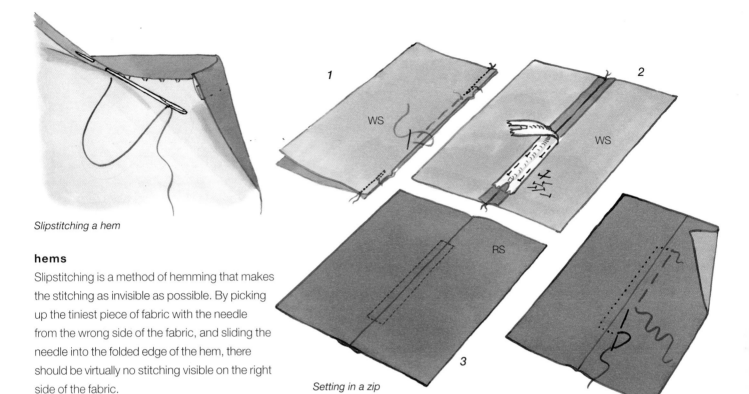

Slipstitching a hem

hems

Slipstitching is a method of hemming that makes the stitching as invisible as possible. By picking up the tiniest piece of fabric with the needle from the wrong side of the fabric, and sliding the needle into the folded edge of the hem, there should be virtually no stitching visible on the right side of the fabric.

fastenings

ZIPS

A zip makes a very practical fastening for an embroidered cushion cover, allowing it to be removed quickly and easily for washing.

Pin the seam into which the zip is to be set, matching the notches that mark the position of the zip. Machine stitch from one end of the seam to the notch and reverse stitch to secure. Repeat at the other end of the seam. Adjust the machine stitch to a large basting stitch and sew along the rest of the seam line from notch to notch, closing up the zip opening (1). Alternatively, tack by hand.

Place the closed zip face down on the wrong side of the fabric, in the zip opening position and centred over the seam line. Pin and tack down (2), then turn the fabric to the right side. Using the zipper foot on your machine, stitch the zip into position from the right side of the fabric, pivoting the fabric through 90 degrees at each corner as you go (3). Press the zip opening and remove the tacking threads.

Prick stitch is a useful stitch for setting in zips by hand. It is a small but strong, almost invisible

Setting in a zip

stitch, and can be worked through several layers of fabric – as will be required when setting in a zip. The method is the same as for backstitch (see page 103), but with a space left between each tiny stitch.

BUTTONHOLES

Buttonholes can be stitched either by machine or by hand. To make machine-stitched buttonholes you will need to refer to your sewing machine manual for instructions, because each machine is slightly different.

Hand-stitched buttonholes are neatened using buttonhole stitch. Working from right to left with the point of the needle facing you, take the needle under the raw edge and up through the underside of the fabric at the required distance from the edge. Loop the thread behind both ends of the needle and pull the needle out of the fabric towards the raw edge, pulling the loop taut to cover the raw edge. Continue in this way, keeping the stitches as close together as possible, until you reach the beginning again, then secure the stitches neatly on the underside of the buttonhole.

Prick stitch used to set in a zip

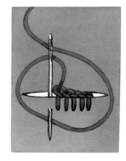

Buttonhole stitch

106

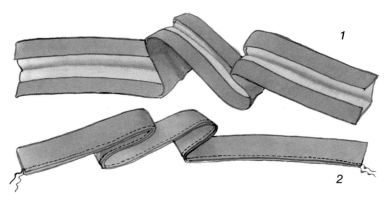

Making loops and ties

LOOPS AND TIES

Several of the projects in this book feature tie fastenings or hanging loops. To make a tie or loop, cut a strip of fabric on the straight grain about 5cm (2in) wide and as long as you want it. When sewn, the tie or loop will be 1.5–2cm (½–¾in) wide. Fold and press the strip of fabric in half lengthways, wrong sides together. Open out the strip and turn in the long raw edges by about 1cm (⅜in) (1). Press. Fold in half again at the centre crease line, wrong sides together. For all the projects in this book, the tie has been knotted 1–2cm in from the edge and then the raw edges cut away close to the knot.

CORDS

A simple fastening can be made by threading a cord through stitched tunnelling and drawing it up tight. Attach a safety pin to one end of the cord. Push the safety pin through one hole of the tunnelling, easing the cord with it, and continue to push it through the tunnelling until the safety pin emerges from the other hole. Wrap a piece of adhesive tape around the cord at the point where you want to cut it. Cut the cord to length in the middle of the adhesive tape, peel off the tape and knot the ends of the cord. Pull the cord to close.

edgings

BIAS TAPE

Bias tape is used for binding raw edges or covering piping cord. It consists of a narrow strip of fabric cut on the cross grain.

To cut out bias strips, first find the bias (cross) grain by folding the straight raw edge of your fabric

at a right angle to the selvedge. Mark and cut out strips across the fabric, parallel to this diagonal line. Join the strips by placing the ends at right angles to each other, right sides together, machine stitching across the join (1).

Press the bias tape in half lengthways, wrong sides together. Open out, then turn in the raw edges so that they almost meet in the middle. Press again.

To apply bias tape to a raw edge, open out the strip and lay one edge of the strip to the raw edge of the fabric, right sides together, placing the bias tape a little way from the edge of the fabric. Stitch along the fold line on the tape (2), turn the tape over to cover the edge of the main fabric, then slip-stitch the other folded edge of the tape in place (3).

Alternatively, you can buy ready-made bias binding in a variety of widths and colours.

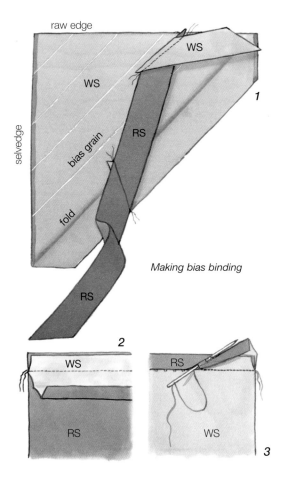

Making bias binding

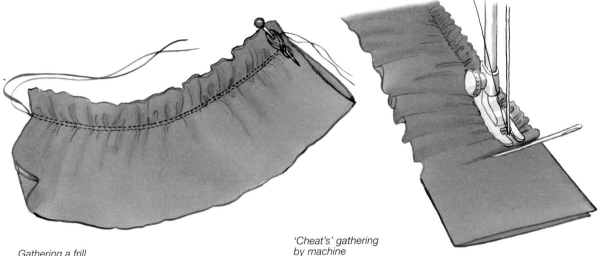

Gathering a frill

*'Cheat's' gathering
by machine*

FRILLS

Gathering can be done by either hand or machine. To gather a frill by hand, use a thread long enough to allow you to gather each section in one go. Run two rows of small, evenly spaced running stitches along the length to be gathered, about 0.5cm (¼in) outside the seam line. To gather a frill by machine, use the largest stitch and follow the method for hand gathering.

To gather, insert a pin at one end of the stitching lines and wind the threads around it, then pull the threads gently from the other end to gather. Repeat at the opposite end.

There is also a 'cheat's' way of gathering long frills by machine. Place the strip of fabric under the machine foot and, using the largest machine stitch, gather the fabric by pushing it under the sewing foot with a needle as you sew. The stitches will hold the gathers in place while the fabric travels under the sewing foot. Sew at a steady and rhythmic pace to achieve even gathers. The gathered frill will not be an exact size, so make more than required and cut to length when the gathering is complete.

mounting pictures

The Windmill Picture and Willow Pattern Sampler (see pages 86 and 88) have been made up into framed pictures, but in fact many of the designs in this book would lend themselves to this treatment. You can take your finished work to a professional for framing, but it is relatively easy to frame your embroideries yourself.

Cut a piece of acid-free mounting board to the size of your picture frame and place it at the back of your embroidery. Secure the embroidery with masking tape on two facing sides. Using a large needle and strong thread, lace the fabric edges together across the back of the board with herringbone stitch. Work outwards from the middle of each side, gently pulling the stitches taut. Repeat the process for the other two sides, first tucking in the spare fabric at the corners.

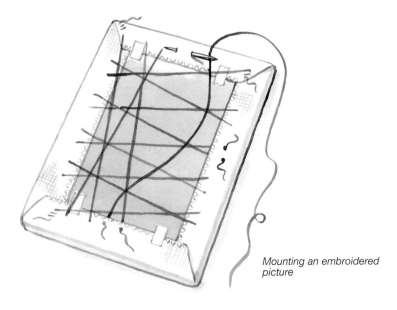

*Mounting an embroidered
picture*

templates

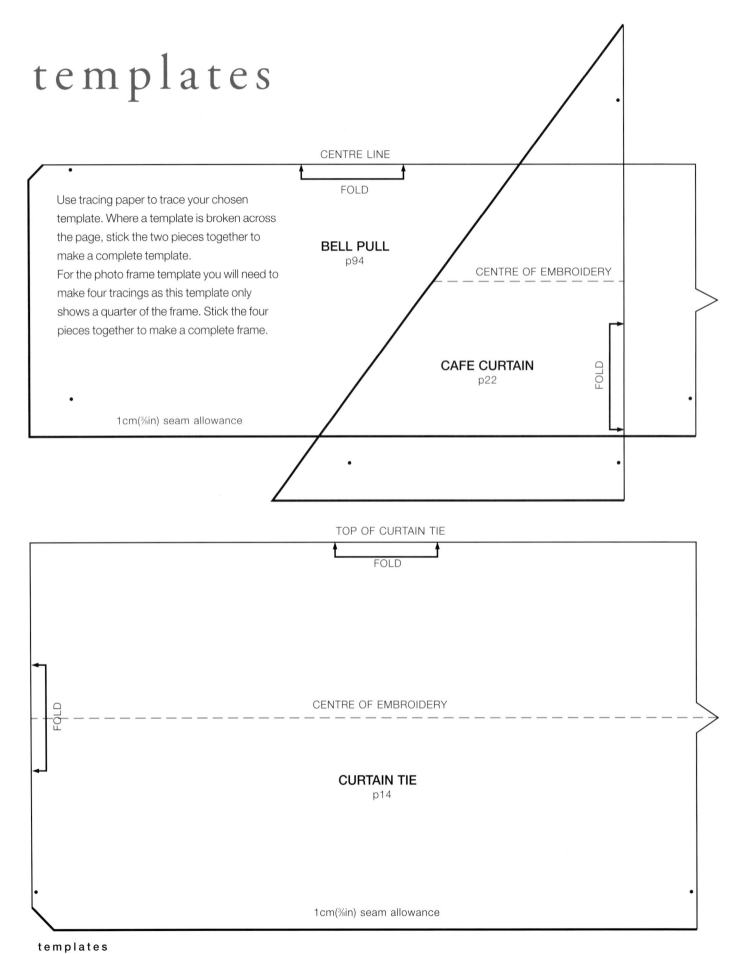

CENTRE LINE

FOLD

Use tracing paper to trace your chosen template. Where a template is broken across the page, stick the two pieces together to make a complete template.
For the photo frame template you will need to make four tracings as this template only shows a quarter of the frame. Stick the four pieces together to make a complete frame.

BELL PULL
p94

CENTRE OF EMBROIDERY

CAFE CURTAIN
p22

FOLD

1cm(⅜in) seam allowance

TOP OF CURTAIN TIE

FOLD

FOLD

CENTRE OF EMBROIDERY

CURTAIN TIE
p14

1cm(⅜in) seam allowance

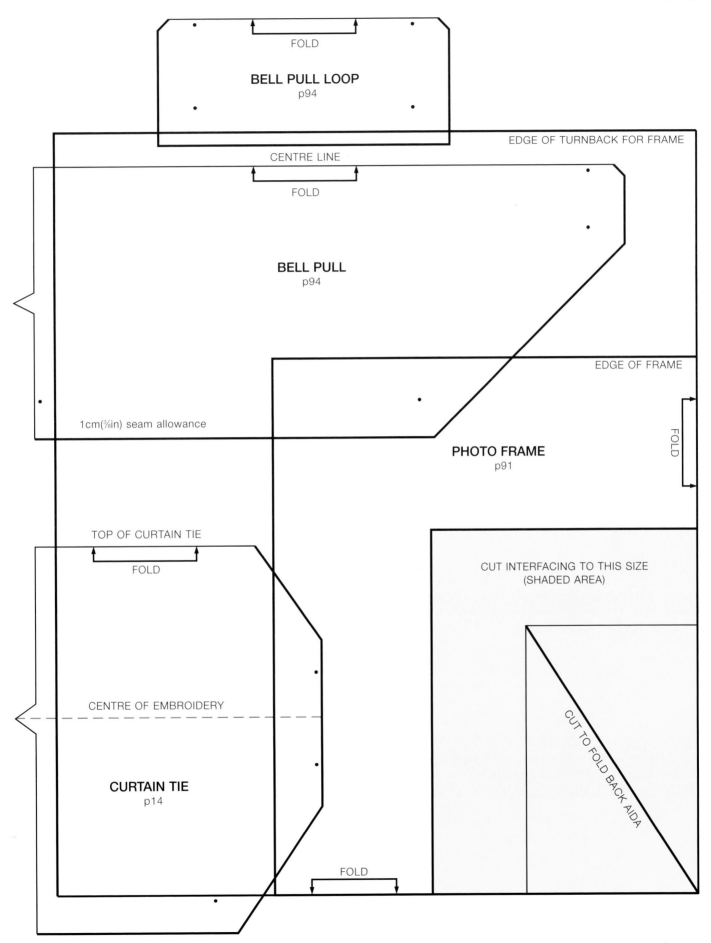

FOLD

BELL PULL LOOP
p94

EDGE OF TURNBACK FOR FRAME

CENTRE LINE

FOLD

BELL PULL
p94

EDGE OF FRAME

1cm(⅜in) seam allowance

FOLD

PHOTO FRAME
p91

TOP OF CURTAIN TIE

FOLD

CUT INTERFACING TO THIS SIZE
(SHADED AREA)

CENTRE OF EMBROIDERY

CUT TO FOLD BACK AIDA

CURTAIN TIE
p14

FOLD

templates

index

acknowledgements

A very special thank you, to Wendy Cockburn for producing beautifully made embroideries for this book. Thank you to my good friends Karen Rowlands and Lorna Cann for lending me a selection of their blue and white pottery for the designs and for the photography. Thank you to Trish for lending me her two Delft tiles and allowing me to draw from some of her rare old dishes.

A big thank you to Cara Ackerman from DMC for sending me all the materials needed for all the projects. Finally, thank you to Alex, my son, for helping me with the computer, and Raymond, my husband, for supporting me when time was precious.

Editor Abi Rowsell
Copy Editor Sarah Widdicombe
Proofreader Alison Bolus
Designer Lisa Tai
Cover Photography Mark Winwood
Photographer Sandra Lane
Illustrator Kate Simunek
Chart artwork Raymond Turvey
Picture Researcher Jennifer Veall
Production Controller Louise Hall

The publisher would like to thank those companies who generously loaned materials and props for the location photography.

pages 20/21,
Graham & Green,
4, 7 & 10 Elgin Crescent,
London W11
Telephone 0207 229 9717

pages 69,74,81
Cologne & Cotton,
Head Office Mail Order,
74 Regent Street,
Leamington Spa,
Warwickshire CV32 4NS
Telephone 01926 332573

pages 35, 37
Ceramica Blue,
10 Blenheim Crescent
London W11 1NN
http://www.ceramicablue.co.uk

pages 9, 26
The Colonial Outpost,
Portobello Road
London W11
http://www.indiajane.co.uk